East-West Dialectics, Currency Resets & the Convergent Power of One

Norman Ball

Preface

This three-part series attempts a vaguely Christian read of the so-called 'East-West dialectic' first by exploring the overarching engine of historical advance (usury and debt-money creation); then onto Russia and China's expanding and consensual roles in global power consolidation before reviewing how the impending currency reset levers power away from the Anglo-American empire (the last empire) towards an ostensible 'multi-lateral system' which, as it turns out, is the penultimate phase of New World Order consolidation.

Some related essays are included from 'the last great financial crisis of 2008' era just to stir the pot further.

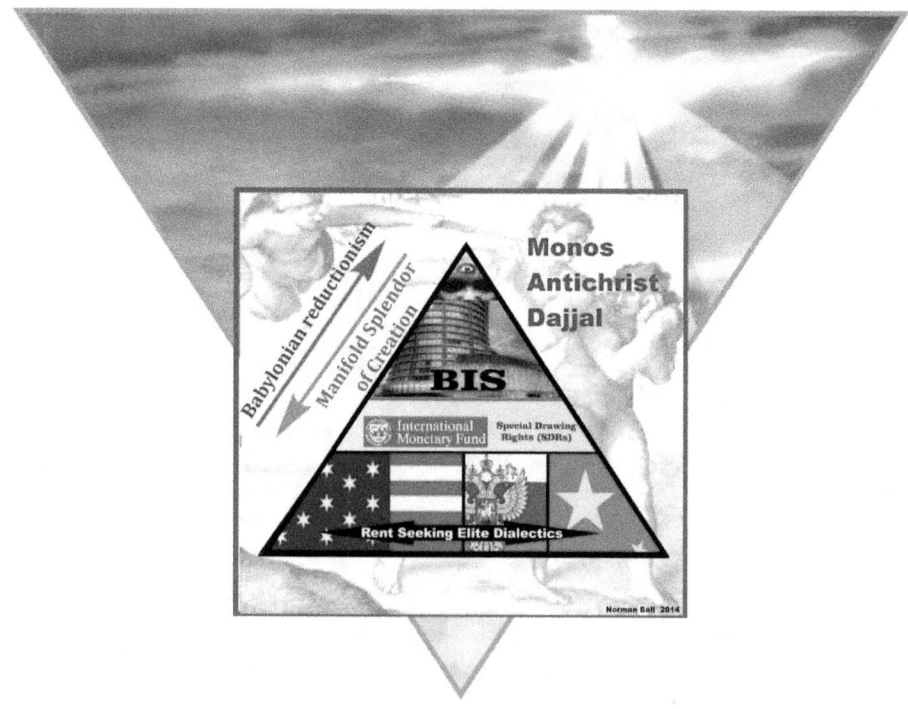

East-West Dialectics, Currency Resets
& the Convergent Power of One

By Norman Ball

Introduction by Carlo Parcelli

GIANT STEPS PRESS
Freeport NY 2013

www.giantstepspress.blogspot.com

eBook prepared, published
& eBook cover desing
by Paul Toth at
Eye Am Eye Books
www.eyeameye.org

Ball, Norman, 1961-

ISBN-13: 978-1508503187
ISBN-10: 1508503184

Printed in The United States of America.
Book design by Norman Ball
Cover design by Norman Ball
gspressnow@gmail.com

Certain 'underlinings' appear throughout the printed
version of the book, denoting linkable URL's in the eBook
version. A subsequent print version will eliminate these.

Contents

Dedicated to my son, Gregory

Introduction

The poet, Ezra Pound, opens his Canto XLV:

"With Usura

With usura hath no man a house of good stone"

His wretched anti-Semitism and pro-Fascist sympathies aside, there can be little doubt that Pound was not wrong about the deleterious effects of usury, its ability to create wealth without commensurate production. Besides, as Norman Ball points out in this short but extraordinarily ambitious volume, the kind of production that would be required to de facto reduce derivatives debt alone would in turn accelerate global ecological devastation. Thus prudent prescriptions at this late stage would precipitate an apocalyptic tailspin far swifter than today's slide toward a secular end-times.

The moral and religious condemnations of usury aside, Mr. Ball's book is no theological screed. No matter how dark, 'East-West Dialectics' is a sober appraisal of the current state of the world economy and the institutions that run it by one who is thoroughly versed in its many facets. There's no evocation of Christ among the money changers here. Facet by facet and with great concision, Ball convincingly argues that the world economy is coming apart at the seams and that the planet's long history of usury, creating wealth from nothing, is the culprit.

In the first part of 'East-West Dialectics', Mr. Ball clearly lays out the connection between 'usury' and the collateral damage of population and planetary dissolution. In the latter part of the book's first section and into the second and third sections, Mr. Ball deftly moves from the eschatological dimension of 'usury' to international jockeying between the US and Britain, Russia and China over which nation-state, or multipolar confluence, will wear the ultimate garland of 'Destroyer of Worlds'. He writes convincingly that the US as unipolar power has already exported itself out of contention, and is in all likelihood, the last empire on the way to the fabled New World Order.

Mr. Ball's writing even about a subject as dry as world economics is vibrant, often brilliant and occasionally dazzling. He brings wit and Swiftian irony to a very grim and difficult topic. All this plus a profound and convincing argument for why we are faced with a modern secular end-times in the age that promised to be a scientific/ technological Utopia.

--Carlo Parcelli, Editor of FlashPoint Magazine and Author, The Canaanite Gospel, A Meditation on Empire: 88 Monologues

Part One: E Pluribus *Monos*

"Just above the disorganized masses, but underneath the Money Changers, exists another demographic which we have referred to as the rent seeking elite. This rent seeking elite attempts to transfer the wealth of the larger masses through processes of taxation and currency manipulation, such as inflation and fractional banking practices.

Once the wealth is consolidated within the smaller demographic, the Money Changers can effectively manage both groups by controlling the money supply on a supra-macro level."

—from Philosophy of Metrics blog

Presently, the United States, Russia and China are engaged in an intricate dance which is the subject both of keen speculation and profound misinterpretation. This three-part series will attempt to examine the forces and inter-class struggles operating both *above* and *within* the so-called East-West dialectic as well as to acknowledge the typically unacknowledged though ubiquitous ether within which all planetary power struggles must unfold. That ether is usury which, in addition to having the world's productive exertions by the throat, orchestrates and encourages horizontal struggle as a means to creating further debt and consolidating vertical power.

Usury is conducted by class. Class obscures itself to better extend usurious advance. As the prefatory quote suggests, we live within a tripartite class system which the popular imagination routinely mistakes for a binary construct. The latter characterization is reinforced by Alex Jones and his ilk's 'Illuminati-versus-little guy' formulation. Relentlessly belaboring the Illuminati trope (complete with well-connected old men cavorting naked around a flaming papier-mâché Owl) Jones *et al* obscure a crucial division within the power structure by implying the elite is more a monolithic overclass than a two-tiered arrangement designed to diffuse perceptions and create an expendable rump of visible elites.

Marx skirts this tripartite arrangement as well with his bourgeois-proletariat two-class structure. However, journalist Ferdinand Lundberg approximates it in his distinction between Financial Politicians (FinPols) and Public Politicians (PubPols). (From Lundberg's 'The Rich and the Super-Rich' (1968): "Finpols and pubpols are generally bedfellows, the latter probably the more ardent in the relationship.") Orwell's Inner Party-Outer Party arrangement in '1984' is another accurate representation.

In order for the people to exploit this gap, they would require media narratives revealing its existence. However, a candid accounting is unlikely as diversionary narratives are the mainstay of mass media. As for what people are being diverted *from*, that would be a singular and concerted power Woodrow Wilson called, "…so organized, so subtle, so watchful, so interlocked, so complete, so pervasive, that [the biggest men in business] had better not speak above their breath when they speak in condemnation of it." This power's pervasiveness has only increased over the ensuing century.

Usury (Islam calls it *riba*) obtains a terrific foothold on human activity by way of debt-money. Certainly there's no more pernicious form of usury than a government allowing private banking interests to use the former's full faith and credit to create society's money. The compulsoriness of this usury arrangement stems from the fact that debt-money is legal tender. We must accept it (by government fiat) for goods and services offered and received. The reason for debt-money's 'hyphenation' is because, like a Janus coin, debt is money and money is debt. This is not readily intuitive. Activist Damon Vrabel explains it this way: "All money comes from the Federal Reserve's private banking system by putting the US government, i.e. 308,000,000 Americans, in debt. If the US government were not in debt to the banking system, the American people would have no money."—from 'The Coming Crash: Usury and the Irrelevant Church'

Thus the first important point about usury in a debt-money system is that we are all implicated in its existence and perpetuation. The principal of usury has invaded our daily currency, which is to say it has overwhelmed the fabric of our lives. There are numerous detailed treatments about the nature of the Federal Reserve and the creation of debt-money such as Paul Grignon's 'Money as Debt' as well as Vrabel's excellent online video documentary 'Renaissance 2.0: Financial Empire'.

We're reminded of the riddle of the Big Bang and cosmic inflation: If the universe is expanding, what is it expanding *into*? This *ex nihilo* mystery mirrors the appearance of debt-money *from where no money was before*. There is no discernible exertion, no labor, beyond a keystroke at a bank. Money is not there. Then it is. Immediately upon its appearance, cash becomes a bank asset and a liability claim is asserted on *We the People*.

Sovereign money, by contrast, is the form of money that has predominated throughout history. Issued by the government, sovereign money pays down debt with no reduction in the money supply. So a key instability (and usury's primary leverage) is removed from the system. Another important point is that debt in a debt-money system is never extinguished, but merely transferred since debt can only be paid off by, well, more debt-money. Keith Weiner offers a neat summary of this phenomenon here on Zero Hedge. Regular people are apt to complain of the Federal Government's deficit spending: 'If I ran my household like this, I wouldn't last long.' Alas, this is a flawed analogy which few media sources rush in to correct. Confusion and collusion are the hallmarks of debt-money discussions.

Again, books have been written on this subject and, incredibly, the very nature of money is still controversial and debated by academics. So we won't belabor it here, except to point out that private banks who preside over the 'birth' of this *ex nihilo* debt-money enjoy the exorbitant privilege of extracting rents from something which amounts to little more than an electronic figment. The societal power that accrues to the debt-money makers is staggering, as well as endlessly replicative with no prior equal for power consolidation on earth.

To be fair, loan activity begins to yield economic benefits as debt-money ripples through a fractional reserve system. By the way, credit and debt are the same thing, just on different sides of the loan process—when credit is extended, debt is incurred. But even as units of account are tallied (to be captured or stored in the value of assets on a corporate balance sheet, for instance), the resultant asset values are little more than conditional liabilities since, in the event of a systemic deflation caused by banks (the agents of 'International Capital', a more fitting term used throughout in place of the prefatory quote's 'Money Changers') extracting their capital from a nation or society—perhaps to deploy it in a more attractive return-on-capital (ROC) nation—money scarcity (capital flight) ensues. Asset values collapse or vanish altogether (the latter, extreme case being hyper-deflation). The wielding of inflationary-deflationary cycles is another conveyor of wealth from bottom to top.

In a globalized economy the rapidity of this capital extraction process can result in wrenching liquidity crises for any nation unfortunate enough to run afoul of International Capital's ROC expectations. We need only look to Greece and its current struggles with the European troika over the former's crippling debt burden. In essence the country is being punished for its capital-unfriendly (leftist) election. Some would argue this is *precisely* the way the system should work. Greece should do a better job of courting International Capital. The more important point is that the state becomes little more than a central bank depot. International Capital arrives and departs like an imperious *ex deus machina* answerable only to the 'sovereign' dictates of investment returns. In a perverse reversal (or rather a brazen revelation of the *monos* doctrine) banking interests come before societal ones. Who's serving whom? We are beginning to see. As economist Henry C. K. Liu puts it: "Reversing the logic that a sound banking system should lead to full employment and developmental growth, BIS regulations demand high unemployment and developmental degradation in national economies as the fair price for a sound global private banking system."

Expanding on Liu's observation of the 'developmental degradation' (drag on growth) the banking edifice imposes on the productive economy, we should remember banks create debt-money but not the interest required to service the ever-mounting legacy debt that accrues. Interest must be hunted down either predatorily from less capital-efficient market participants achieving lesser returns (competition), captured through increased economies of scale and acquisition (the *monos*-friendly concentration of power) or extracted through further predations on the environment.

Thus economic growth bears a dual burden. It must service the accumulating debt in existence *and* enlarge the economy, thereby forging fresh havens for debt-money. Society has been schooled on the mantra of growth (sustainment is a bad word to the bankers). However growth is not a given, historically speaking. Satyajit Das, author of 'Traders Guns & Money' offers some astonishing data on that <u>exceedingly rare economic phenomenon called organic growth</u> [my underline]: "Between 1500 and 1820, economic production increased by less than 2% <u>per century</u>. Between 1820 and 1900, economic production roughly doubled. Between 1901 and 2000, economic production increased by a factor of something like four times."

So does the modern economy deserve a congratulatory pat on the back for relegating slow-no growth to the Dark Ages? Not so fast. The amount of debt required to squeeze growth from the economy is increasing. Das goes on: "By 2008, $4 to $5 of debt was required to create $1 of growth. China now needs $6 to $8 of credit to generate $1 of growth, an increase from around $1 to $2 of credit for every $1 of growth a decade ago."

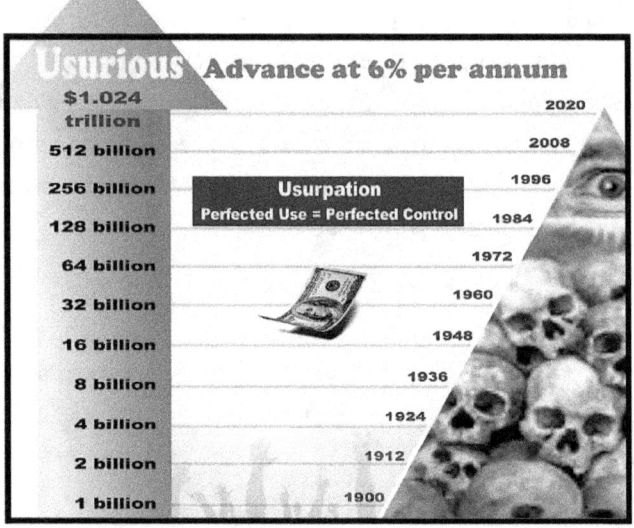

Das attributes the superstructure of financialization for this gravity-defying wizardry. With its fondness for exotic acronyms and the amassing of too-large numbers that resist any real-world correlatives (Ellen Brown estimates the notional value of the derivatives complex at <u>$1.2 quadrillion or 20 times the combined GDP of the planet</u>), financialization can best be called charlatanism. Of course, the Rent Seeking Elite's power and prestige rests on this teetering edifice. International Capital, with its centuries-long vantage, knows financialization is dressed-up chicanery. This Ponzi too shall pass, though with catastrophic societal results.

There's every reason to believe the nation-state won't survive the carnage. This, in a nutshell, is where the New World Order comes in. Even if it wasn't explicitly planned, the NWO would be necessitated by the law of large numbers. The scale, extent and uniformity of the debt crisis across all nations argues for a supranational convergence point. Certainly this will be the argument used to internationalize human affairs further. Capital is shaping the world in its image.

No less than Albert Einstein conceded: "Compound interest is the eighth wonder of the world. He who understands it, earns it; he who doesn't, pays it." Alas the future pays it too. Any activity that, quite literally, borrows from the future in order to enrich the present is a moral trespass. Usury lies somewhere between weird alchemy and illicit time machine. The future is not here to assert its claims, and too few present-day humans seem willing to forgo their ill-gotten consumption for a bunch of folk who do not yet exist and perhaps never will. We might call this the jealous prerogative of the present, really a generational crowding-out effect. The yet-to-live don't have sharp elbows because they don't have elbows. Human decency should allow them a seat at the table nonetheless.

Usury is the teleological machine within God's overarching eschatology that drives the doomed mission of International Capital. This group is really the 'upper house chamber' of our bicameral elite. Wearing the mantle of Babel and resisting ready characterization, International Capital directs the manufactured narratives that inform the passions of the people, yet scrupulously avoids an overt speaking role for itself. Its presence is felt everywhere.

However, no graven images are allowed. Invisibility obscures culpability. Headless villains are not readily summoned to the gallows. International Capital's hired hands, the ever-so mercenary Rent Seeking Elite, exist to handle all the flak and occupy the noose-end of the occasional public hangings as required.

The fact is International Capital can well afford to rise above the crisis *du jour* atmosphere put on by the Rent Seeking Elite—the latter being not so much crisis managers as crisis purveyors. That's how unbridgeable the wealth gap has become. Through a strange admixture of math, mystery and supernatural impartation, usury has delivered the world to an abyss that purports to be a pinnacle. (This essay is sure to exasperate all parties as it weaves from the geopolitical to the supernatural to the conspiratorial and back again. All roads narrow into one when the consecrating capstone of the pyramid lies straight ahead— or is it directly above?) Bluntly, monetary policy is a Babelian force with a spiritual agenda [underline added]: "The suggested relation singles out a correspondence between a religion, <u>which tends to reduce the manifold to the monos (One), and the economic forms (usury)</u> organized by a culture that manifests itself as reduction." —'<u>Machine Art and Other Writings: The Lost Thought of the Italian Years: Ezra Pound</u>' from Introduction by Maria Luisa Ardizzone

The indefatigable power of numbers, an inhuman (*contra naturam*) force that will one day throw off even those hubristic few who presume to ride its back, is impervious to human countermeasure. International Capital is more force than personage anyway—a Minotaur destined to shed

12

all human vestige at the end. The vagaries of humanity fill the demoniac with contempt. Man is an expedient vehicle for Satan and nothing more. No human will survive the pitiless edifice for long, save for one: the Antichrist (or for our Muslim friends, the Dajjal). Even this uneasy consummation of Man and Beast will be short-lived.

The Rent Seeking Elite masticates the gathered fruits of Labor before siphoning off a handsome (though comparatively negligible) surcharge for its collection and custodial duties. International Capital then slurps the indeterminate soup of capitalized labor upwards to be re-deployed anywhere in the world, without compunction, and only as return on capital dictates. As truck drivers from Duluth realized instinctively about NAFTA, free trade is all about the unimpeded flow of capital and the marginalization of Labor. Finally, the term Labor carries with it some anachronistic Marxist baggage. In this information age creative-intellectual inspiration forms no less extractive a labor output as manning an industrial assembly line. The exploitive paradigm is the same. As the Timing Logic blog reminds us: "All labor is exploited whether it is physical labor or intellectual labor."

The horizontal dialectics perpetrated by warring elites are loosely monitored by International Capital which sits astride all conflict with Darwinian resign. Friction yields return on capital. War debt consolidates in an upward fashion. Usury need not concern itself with the minutiae of world events because it is the magnetic pole to which all events move. The exponential power of compounding interest is such that the world cannot help but converge on monistic consolidation. In the fullness of time, the All-Seeing Eye with have it All.

This inhuman drive towards the *monos* is both at odds and yet entirely consistent with God's plan. *Come, let us.* The implicit entreaty that starts Genesis 11:19 denotes a whispered few *conspiring* to sequester themselves from both God and greater mankind with an ulterior project of sufficient devious construct that it will ensnare and bedevil Man for the full term of human history: "Come, let us build ourselves a city, with a tower that reaches to the heavens, so that we may make a name for ourselves; otherwise we will be scattered over the face of the whole earth."

The Tower is the world's monetary edifice. The name they make for themselves is variously known as Luciferianism or Babylonianism. Mammon is their god. Banking is their *modus operandi.* By confusing men with a variety of tongues God furnishes the Babylonians with a tactical advantage in their usury-advancing schemes that will soon include pitting neighbor against neighbor, sewing internal discord and conspiring between nations to foment the debt-bonanza called war. The New World Order is a thus a wine from Man's vineyard sold before God's time. Nations exist by virtue of His scattering, not to be united until Jesus returns. George Soros wants to usher in the New World Order. He's not getting any younger you know. God's sense of timing is less advertised.

Jesus, in His most heated moment, symbolically interrupts Mammon's usurious advance by overturning (resetting?) the former's ledgers and accounts in the Temple. Knowing full well this is the nemesis He will face at the full apogee of its power in the Final Days, He summons up a passion fully commensurate to the primacy of the threat.

Everyman prurience gravitates to the Hollywood trope of a personalized demon—a Dr. No. This comfortable enemy diverts from the featureless, pitiless 'heart' of International Capital, the real (and ultimately soulless) foe of all humanity. All ethnicities and nationalities are implicated in these monetary flights of fancy. The earliest paper money can be traced to 7th century China where its habitual inflation caused the ruin of many dynasties. How ironic that today's China should find itself stuffed to the gills with electronic USDs once removed even from paper fiat. In a recent on-line interview Modern Monetary Theory (MMT) pioneer Warren Mosler underlines the profound surreality of the situation [at 20:31]: "all [the Chinese] have are data on the Fed's computer...they've traded all these goods and services for just numbers on the Fed's spreadsheet."

Chinese predecessors notwithstanding, as Ezra Pound insisted, "we are concerned with the vagaries of the Western World" (from 'What Is Money For?'). In 1694, fellow Scotsman Sir William Paterson, founder of the Bank of England, won approval from King William III to create bank notes as exclusive English legal tender. Paterson would say, "the bank hath profit on the interest of all the moneys which it creates out of nothing." Today, monetary reform activist Damon Vrabel describes International Capital simply as 'senior capital pools of inter-generational wealth'. For my money, that's label enough.

The wielders of International Capital are not the mere billionaires we are familiar with; the media-enamored *nouveau riche* who populate *Forbe*'s Richest Men in the World lists. We are instead in the rarified realm of multi-trillionaires whose wealth is stored in vast networks of corporate entities, LLC's and 'off-the-grid' (currency-independent) art, collectibles, gems and precious metals. Having witnessed if not outright engineered over the centuries the unanimous debasement of fiat currencies, these entities, one can guess, hold vast storehouses of gold as well. Fiats are crucial conveyors of wealth from the bottom to the top, administered of course by the Rent Seeking Elite. In fact the filthy secret of fiat currency is that it serves mostly to engender initial (misplaced) trust before emptying the storehouse with inflation. The masses offer labor. They are rewarded in the end with destitution.

Legal tender laws codify and enforce the conversion of society's productive energies into fool's gold. The poor, having no recourse beyond fiat, are fated to lose everything. Usury works like a trans-generational ratchet, escaping the boom-bust cycle by closing the teller window at opportune times. In this way the rich get richer while the rest enjoy brief interludes of prosperity punctuated by deflationary collapse or hyperinflationary vaporization. Money is a thief disguised as a storehouse.

Central bankers, a crucial inter-class intermediation point, are careful to denigrate gold at every turn. This advertised aversion speaks volumes. Transcending time and space, usury passes through successive empires like a restless, ever-onward-and-upward spirit with worldly ambitions as unmatchable as its earthly dominion is, during this period we call history, unassailable.

This age-old boom-bust cycle has sewn dysfunction into the collective mass psyche. Anxiety seeds inaction, as the masses feel paralyzed and powerless while those who sit astride International Capital enjoy an inoculated existence befitting gods on earth. The latter's control can afford to be more circumspect than despotic as centuries of usury have extinguished all credible pretenders to the throne. Their lead, in short, is insurmountable.

By contrast, we who live down below contend within the vortex of history and its purposeful favoring of extremes. The world is made to feel more dangerous than it is, its resources more scarce. Social resistance, when it isn't organized opposition, becomes promptly infiltrated and turned around. Manufactured consent is leavened with bogeymen, perma-war and the threat of imminently invading aliens. The very few govern the very many through paralytic fear, endless diversion and oceans of money.

Creatures of circumstance, Rent Seeking Elites are lashed to the Empires they serve. The sandwiched class, they constitute in many ways the dregs of mankind as they have no transcendent historic purpose. Mercenary in the extreme and compelled by avarice, power-lust and sexual deviance (a useful currency of extortion and control), they believe in very little beyond their own mortal, ego-driven *petit* power games. Hunter S. Thompson was only half-right when he suggested scum rises. It does. But only to the middle of the jar. The Rent Seeking Elite are a no-mans' land of humanity's least coveted traits. As Orwell said of the inner party-outer party demarcation: "All the smart dummies, upper class and yuppies go along with and/or join the Outer Party thinking they'll win, when the Inner Party hates them more than the proles.

For lack of a better descriptor the Rent Seeking Elite generally alluded to as the 'West' within the East-West dialectic and the preferred vehicle of International Capital is what this essay will call the Anglo-Americans. Very broadly, this elite consists of vestiges of the British Empire, the military industrial complex, multinational corporations, the media establishment, the New York and London financial and banking complex, a Deep State amalgam of security and intelligence interests, the NATO arc within Western Europe, in other words, a confederacy of interlocking interests bound by Anglo-Saxon and Zionist exceptionalist and Manifest Destiny precepts and a distinct sense of Empire whose titular locus is the US Government. This Empire enforces Pax Americana which is financed by the reserve and petrodollar currency status of the US Dollar.

Western Europe, so often accused today of being a vassal entity of the Anglo-American Empire is indeed a region of influence within the Empire's arc, though once-removed from the Empire itself. In this context, NATO is not so much a cooperative alliance with a command structure as an occupying military presence within Europe that would likely offer resistance were Germany, for example, to formally pivot towards Russia and Eurasia where arguably its economic destiny lies. National Front party leader Marine Le Pen's recent expressed desire to have France leave NATO has perhaps been relegated to the dustbin with the *Charlie Hebdo* attack in Paris. It would have been interesting to see how such an effort might evolve.

As for the Deep State element of the Anglo-American Empire, Peter Dale Scott's book 'Deep Politics and the Death of JFK' is the source document. In a recent Voltairenet interview, Scott characterizes the Deep State as:

> "a wide zone or milieu of interaction between the public state and unseen dark forces... a parallel secret government, organized by the intelligence and security apparatus, financed by drugs, and engaging in illicit violence, to protect the status and interests of the military against threats from intellectuals, religious groups, and occasionally the constitutional government."

Thus the Deep State is a shadow element within the Anglo-American Empire seeking to accomplish certain empire objectives that contradict the explicit democratic principles of the Public State; a structurally sanctioned internal contradiction, in short.

Great media effort is expended to sustain the impression that the Anglo-American Empire is really nothing more or less than the US Government working on behalf of the American people for discretely American interests. In fact the Anglo-American Empire serves the transcendent interests of International Capital as did the empires that preceded it. Furthermore, these interests are often antithetical to purely American ones. Thus one key role of media is to conflate the two and manufacture domestic consent for internationalist objectives.

The prerogatives of empire rendered America and its citizens oddly incidental if not hostage to the USD and the military industrial complex as the latter were conscripted away from parochial (national) responsibilities to better serve an internationalist agenda. In some sense the Triffin Paradox has in fact relinquished its paradox by jettisoning its domestic responsibilities. (The Triffin Paradox is created by the demand on an international currency requiring an excess supply that tends to undermine its role as a national currency due to the need for the reserve country to run a permanent current accounts deficit.) America is alone among nations in that it does not have an answerable national currency. What the Philosophy of Metrics blog calls below a <u>'supra-sovereign banking structure'</u> is in essence International Capital:

> We haven't lived in a US dominated world for the last 70 years, it only appears that way. We have lived in a supra-sovereign banking structure which used the USD system and American military to expand its reach. Now this same supra-sovereign banking structure is transitioning from a USD reserve system to a SDR reserve system.

If it can be said the rich are different, then surely the super-rich approximate an alien species in our midst. Even today, International Capitalists almost certainly observe a spiritual and ritualized praxis of ancient design. A belief system ensures inter-generational discipline while insulating against defeatist behaviors brought on by dissipation. Importantly, they see no evil in their worldview. On the contrary, they are the fruit of mankind and the rightful inheritors of earth. The Bible, they would argue, demonizes them (Gnosticism exposes the demiurge masquerading as Yahweh, for example) in order to fulfill its own twisted ends.

Thus to the many well-intentioned social activists out there engrossed in their endless fund-raising drives, the message is that the struggle for *world dominion on earth* is a *fait accompli*. Usury is conceptually pitted against social justice. International Capital won, not because the pitchforks failed to prick the proper enemy in time, but because this age belongs to Mammon by God's implicit 'blessing'. International Capital, through the auspices of The Bank of International Settlements (BIS) and the International Monetary Fund (IMF) is now engaged in consolidating a centuries-long ascent towards monetary hegemony. (Many readers, secularists especially, will recoil at the ascetic passivity of this account, thinking Marx' famous opiate has dulled my sense of injustice. What can I say? Eschatology feeds contentedly resigned fatalism.)

On to more earthbound vexations—gold is a good place to vex as it is perpetually embroiled in an identity crisis both within itself and with the world at large. What is gold exactly? An element? An aesthetically pleasing, yet barbarous relic? A monetary departure-point for fiat hijinks? Jim Rickards believes gold is on the verge of reasserting its traditional monetary identity. No other power on earth casts sand in the eye of fiat currencies and monetary policy by virtue simply of its existence as does gold. As monetary scientist Antal Fekete likes to remind us, gold, the great *a priori* storehouse of value, is not priced in fiat. Fiat is priced in gold. Similarly, those who are not *of* the world lie *beyond* the world's control. Thus the doubly-charged evocative power of William Jennings Bryan's 'cross of gold' becomes all too clear.

In a recent blog entry, Rickards imagines the fate of gold in the year 2024 after it has been confiscated and placed in a Swiss vault by the world government:

> The purpose of the Swiss vault was not to have gold backing for currencies, but rather to remove gold from the financial system entirely so it could never be used as money again. Thus, gold trading ceased because its production, use and possession were banned. By these means, the G-20 and the World Central Bank control the only forms of money.

Rickards stops short of tracing the full arc of his implied *telos*. In fact all forms of money will perish when perfect control is achieved. Act One was the curtains coming down on price discovery in 2008 with the Fed's implementation of Quantitative Easing. The markets, controlled by our Rent Seeking Elite, now dictate 'auctionless value' in true command economy style. Value has been severed from the democratic scrum. This contributes to grassroots alienation, powerlessness and despair. In the future, currency as a medium of exchange will be replaced with a mark signaling complete submission. We will exchange fealty for food and shelter. The currency of survival will be uncomplaining servitude to the One.

Gold and the human soul share an alchemical affinity. This is just as well since Christians will fare no better than the shiny metal under the New World Order. The latter will be absolutely fastidious in its tyranny with no patience for

22

even token dissent. Why? Unparalleled self-regard necessitates unblemished submission: "The realized one is such that it has only itself before itself, and as such excludes any otherness."—from Theorie-Werkausgabe, Georg Wilhelm Friedrich Hegel

In the novel *1984*, the state knows it is not enough simply to arrest Winston or even to kill him. The system's cherished conceit of internal consistency (perfect control) is imperiled if Winston's 'consent' is not willingly offered up. There will be an apologist like Dick Cheney to insist Room 101 is not so much a terror vestibule as an enhanced interrogation facility where people are assisted towards resolving their internal contradictions in a manner consistent with the state's *a priori* conviction that it is in fact omnipotent. Omnipotence, impossible on earth anyway, cannot abide contradiction as that is tantamount to denying the reality of its own existence. Alastair Crooke points out, in the context of lessons learned by Sunni intellectuals in the wake of the Soviet defeat in Afghanistan, a possible recipe for Empire resistance:

> Thus, they devised a calibrated action plan intended to provoke and "sting" the West into hasty—and hugely costly—military over-reaction; into blatant contradictions of their own "narrative" of benevolence, freedom and democracy; and into the fragmentation of their own internal cohesion through the deliberate playing upon Western internal contradictions—

and the exposing of "the illusion" of US omniscience.

The condition of omnipotence has teleological implications as it necessitates the prior resolution of all dialectical conflicts. Winston's false consciousness harks back to an older, pre-resolved world. Didn't he get the Basel III memo? On some conceptual level, he does not exist if he cannot be convinced of his historical obsolescence, then 'brought forward' of his own volition. Equally vexing to the state, he cannot be killed if he cannot exist. He is a variant of Rome's *homo sacer*, a man who can neither be sacrificed on the state's sepulcher of omnipotence, nor embraced in his apostate form. Perhaps Rickards foresees a human vault too in some grim future—the Black Iron Prison of Irresolvable Contradictees.

How will the final currency end? Hyper-deflation is an asymptotic phenomenon caused by the rapid removal of money from a society. Some time off yet, money's last gasp will see asset values approaching zero infinitely. This could be how the wealth gap will widen—until it disappears. When *monos* is reached, International Capital will have gathered unto itself the entirety of the world's riches. Owning everything extinguishes valuation, the latter being necessitated only by the prospect of exchange. The super-elite will covet to themselves transhumanist advances such as longevity and disease control. Many transhumanists foresee the extinction of Labor and Capital in a world of abundant leisure. Few extend the implications to their logical conclusion. The bulk of humanity, now completely extraneous, will suffer a benign (perhaps malign) neglect that will see their numbers fall dramatically. The hyperexceptionalist character of those who sit astride International Capital will not allow inter-class sharing of this abundance, even if such largesse is economically and technologically feasible. They will jealously covet it. They alone are destined to enjoy it.

We are approaching this day. Indeed human history was devised to accomplish the near-perfect control paradigm of money wed seamlessly to power. (Full perfection will be thwarted by a handful of obstinate Christians crouched shivering in seemingly godforsaken caves; my Jewish and Muslim friends are well equipped to plead their own cases. There is undoubted theological merit across the Abrahamic sphere.) Usury is all about power. Money is a ladder to be cast down when *monos* is achieved.

We've belabored this tripartite class structure because in order to understand an enemy, one must sometimes identify both of them. The implications of International Capital's tightening noose, and the mop-up operations that are concluding beneath it, are that the dialectics become more compressed, and thus more entangled, than in times past. The *e pluribus unum* pyramid is a convergent structure, the reductive sieve of historic determinism (if not the horn of the Beast itself). Reduction narrows our recourse to freedom. Within seconds, a Socialist victory in a Greek election precipitates a European capital flight to US bond market safety. As the interconnectedness becomes claustrophobic, one discerns the walls of the Panopticon closing in. My hiccup in Kansas causes you to scratch your ear a thousand miles away in Caracas. No one knows why. Yet it happens.

Too often, the argument against usury is freighted with class envy. The sin of usury is not expatiated by substituting the sin of envy. The problem is not that you or I had the ill fortune *not* to be part of the banking elite—or else oh how grand life would be! That's simply the inversion of the cult of personality disease. Usury is an encompassing, malignant spirit that inhabits all classes, assigning to each stratum a separate and discrete sub-task. We are all complicit in usury's relentless progress. The Fall was universal. Scapegoating and class warfare, while perhaps tempting, are ultimately fruitless non-starters.

Nonetheless, we must delve the tripartite class structure that formed around usury, in an effort to understand how this structure assists the consolidation of power on earth. For that is precisely what it is doing. Then we will turn to its present-day machinations, with all dialectical confusions thereunto appertaining, to better gauge the stage of its completion.

Many recoil at the slightest suggestion of overarching conspiracies. Let me warn the reader that this is an eschatological analysis pledged to the most transcendent and overarching conspiracy of all: the Fall of Man, the advent of history and Man's ensuing redemption. Hopefully, this early admission will not scare away non-Christians as this account holds something for them as well. But again, history, in my view, is divinely directed, and will leave behind no unanswered questions when it concludes. The purpose of history, to the extent Man is allowed to know it, centers around allowing the hidden faction alluded to by Woodrow Wilson to amass all worldly power in an impudent (dare we say sacrilegious) attempt to reprise paradise on earth, *imago Dei.*

Part Two: Russia and China - Welcome to Our 'Teleological Dream'

> "The United States, in short, is challenged so to conduct itself as to bridge over in every possible way the potential cleavage between East and West"
>
> --from Prospect for America: The Rockefeller Panel Report (1961)

Part one of this series explored the tripartite class system that girds the world with the engine of usury enforcing the divisions. Part two examines the ascendancy of Russia and China in line with the next phase of International Capital's ever-consolidating advance.

Though furtive and non-interventionist by habit, International Capital does not endorse all dialectical combatants at all times. Sometimes the upper chamber of the elite wants to squash a particular lower chamber's motion. To do this, it may collaborate with one Rent Seeking Elite faction at cost to another. The Anglo-American elite was, until very recently, International Capital's most favored nation, certainly its empiric vehicle. Perhaps the former has failed the challenge laid out by the Rockefeller report prefaced above, or merely expended itself as all empires do. (The same report explicitly notes the thirteen empires the world had seen prior to the turn of the 20th century; there is another theme that the 'system of empires' has fulfilled its historical mission and cannot be resuscitated.) Indeed the relationship is of such longstanding that it assists in the prevalent but erroneous conflating of the two class entities

International Capital's favoritism towards the Anglo-American Empire may be in the midst of a significant downgrade given all that is at stake: potential thermonuclear confrontation, the growing petulance and irrationality of the Anglo-American elite and the better growth opportunities beckoning in every place of the world where this Empire happens not to be. International Capital votes with its feet. The result is a regional capital strike, popularized as 'America's factories being torn down and shipped to Asia.'

Russia is a current flashpoint that helps illumine these ongoing tectonic shifts. By way of illustration, here is a passage from a recent entry at the <u>Vineyard of the Saker</u>:

> I would, however, argue that the biggest threat for Russia is internal, not external. Nothing is more dangerous for the future of Russia than what I call the "Atlantic Integrationists" and which Putin even called the "5th column"...True, these pro-Anglo Zionist 5th columnists have suffered a series of setbacks and they have been weakened by Putin's relentless assault on their power, but what does "weaker" really mean in our context? According to Mikhail Khazin the Eurasian Sovereignists and the Atlantic Integrationists are now roughly at 50/50 in terms of power. That's right, Putin is far from having total control of Russia and he is in fact locked into a war for survival against a formidable foe who will try to

capitalize on every setback Russia suffers, especially in her economy. Putin knows that and he is therefore in a race against time to de-couple Russia from the economic and financial mechanisms which make it possible for the Anglo Zionists to hurt Russia.

Saker is absolutely right regarding the essential internality of the conflict. However he strays into an overly-romanticized depiction frequently encountered in the Russian press. Putin is not a Putinist as the latter is a reductive and folksy characterization not becoming of this shrewd multi-dimensional leader. Yes indeed, he is engaged in a struggle with the so-called Anglo-American Empire; (characterize it as one likes—an activated front within the broader East versus West struggle; Atlantic Integrationists versus Eurasian Sovereignists, which seems the preference of many Russians. Importantly, this is _not_ a dialectical struggle in the strict Hegelian sense as we'll explore later in this essay.) Where Saker's analysis possibly founders is in its unconsidered melding of International Capital and the Anglo-American Rent Seeking Elite as though both class' interests are at all times perfectly correlated. Again, they aren't. This misread cascades further into the assumption that Putin must be opposed to the 'Atlantic Integrationists' in his midst. He isn't.

Though there may be some seditious element within this group with explicit ties to the Anglo-American Empire (though this falls more under the aegis of espionage than dialectics), Atlantic Integrationism is tethered less to the Anglo-American Empire than to the transcendent interests of International Capital itself. And what of the Eurasian

Sovereignists? There is nothing to suggest they are any more loyal to Russian interests than are the Atlantic Integrationists. Indeed there is every reason to believe International Capital is *not* joining the battle against Putin in this instance.

One thinks of a teacher who usually allows his two students to battle their differences out in a schoolyard fight, but on occasion actively eggs one student on against the other. This analogy is instructive only when the tripartite structure is acknowledged and understood. Hence my belabored treatment of it earlier. Believing this also suggests there exists no small amount of bleed-through in the so-called East-West dialectic. In short, there's more than a little west in the east, and some western sovereignist tendencies as well (the Tea Party? UKIP?) This bleed-through is a telltale fingerprint of International Capital working its effects everywhere it is—which is, well, everywhere.

An equally flawed read, this time on the part of Russian ultra-nationalists is that Putin does not fear embarking on a domestic variant of North Korean *juche*. Alas, this too is more Peter the Great grandstanding. Far more likely, Putin is resisting a recalcitrant, overstayed and highly dangerous Anglo-American empire *at the behest* of International Capital. For its part, the latter is attempting to extricate itself from the Anglo-American Empire much as one would a banged-up car at the side of the road.

What evidence is there to suggest that both Russia and China are the emergent favorites in the eyes of International Capital at this time? Who can reasonably argue otherwise? Putin is not 'a leader with a weak hand biding his time until he can deal a blow to the Anglo-Americans who've captured the Russian Central Bank'. That's pure theater. <u>Putin is an avowed integrationist.</u> Russia is neither pivoting east nor west. Both it and China are movin' on up with some level of coordination, that is, up the pyramid of International Capital to fill the gap created by the estrangement of the Anglo-Americans with the IMF, a titular institution beholden not to the US—as many believe—but to International Capital itself.

Both nations are members of the Bank of International Settlements (BIS). Putin (no less than China's Xi Jinping) has abundantly signaled his endorsement of the IMF (SDR) currency reset and related governance reforms. Here's Putin in <u>July 2014</u>: "[There is a] common intention to reform the international monetary and financial system. In the present form it is unjust to the BRICS countries and to new economies in general. We should take a more active part in the IMF and the World Bank's decision-making system."

And here's China's Central Bank Governor in a <u>2009 essay</u>:

> The world economic crisis shows the "inherent vulnerabilities and systemic risks in the existing international monetary system," Gov. Zhou Xiaochuan said in an essay released Monday by the bank. He recommended creating a currency made up of a basket of global currencies and controlled by the International Monetary Fund and said it would help "to achieve the objective of

safeguarding global economic and financial stability.

It's fitting here also to torpedo the notion that BRICS is anything other than a coordinated step towards full IMF and SDR integration, and not a parallel monetary structure, as has been suggested by some. On this, the <u>Philosophy of Metrics</u> blog has it right:

> The BRICS economies...have expanded the structure of the international financial system by implementing the New Development Bank and Contingency Reserve Arrangement. Most analysts and commenters promote the story that the BRICS countries are going to overthrow the Western banks and implement their own gold backed system.

> This simply is not true or factual as the BRICS countries themselves are demanding reform to the International Monetary Fund, as agreed in 2010 by all 188 members, including the American administration. And China has been quickly internationalizing the RMB for inclusion into the SDR basket composition by next July, a date which quickly follows the next OPEC meeting in June, 2015.

Though the relationship between BRICS and the IMF remains murky, there's little doubt this monetary front has been falsely conscripted into the East-West dialectic, and that the formers' respective missions will be more complementary than contentious. The certainty of global de-dollarization (the necessity of which is further underlined by the USD's current violent upswing and the ensuing carnage to the global economy) has caused ill-considered default camps to form around the Chinese renminbi, BRICS, even an SCO currency-basket monetary alternative, as potential follow-on reserve currencies. As the USD sucks the life out of currencies the world over, this dollar strengthening—deflationary enough by itself—will precipitate an even larger deflation should world economic activity go into a tailspin (46% of S&P 500 earnings are generated overseas.)

In fact the USD will be the last national currency to fulfill the role of world reserve currency. As Robert Triffin argued at the time of Bretton Woods, the divergent roles of a currency acting in both a national and reserve capacity are disruptive and self-contradicting. In 1971, President Nixon 'temporarily' closed the gold window. An argument can be made this 'Bretton Woods default' stripped the dollar of its status as money, relegating it to mere currency and floating medium of exchange. Later, the petrodollar would enhance the qualitative status of the USD by reinstating a measure of value via the flexible oil standard where once there had been a fixed gold standard.

F. William Engdahl's book 'A Century of War' is indispensable to understanding the third and final leg of the USD's colorful and exorbitant life abroad, the petrodollar and petrodollar recycling. Few know that the Arab Oil Embargo which caused a 400% increase in oil prices overnight was instigated, not by Gulf Arab states humiliated at the outcome of the Yom Kippur War, but by International Capital and its banking elite even before the war started:

In May 1973...a group of 84 of the world's top
financial and political insiders met at Saltsjöbaden,
Sweden, the secluded island resort of the Swedish
Wallenberg banking family. This gathering of
Prince Bernhard's Bilderberg group heard an
American participant, Walter Levy, outline a
'scenario' for an imminent 400 per cent increase in
OPEC petroleum revenues. The purpose of the
secret Saltsjobaden meeting was not to prevent
the expected oil price shock, but rather to plan
how to manage the about-to-be-created flood of
oil dollars, a process U.S. Secretary of State
Kissinger later called 'recycling the petrodollar
flows.'—from 'A Century of War', F. William
Engdahl

The effects of petrodollar recycling were manifold.
Developing economies were suddenly faced with huge
energy bills requiring ever more USD's to pay (and
precipitating the third world debt crisis); the onus of
financial power shifted decisively from the productive to
the financial sector of the economy; Anglo-American oil
companies' flagging prospects were boosted overnight; and
the implications of the Triffin Paradox were pushed aside
for another generation. Sheikh Imran Hosein is right to call
petrodollar recycling 'evil genius'. He is also right to accuse
the hapless King Faisal of singlehandedly (and in large part
unwittingly) institutionalizing the largest wealth transfer
from poor Muslim nations to wealthy western nations than
could ever have been dreamt of in the days of colonialism.

Petrodollar recycling peaked in 2006. In fact, the recycling
is projected to turn into 'decycling' for the first time in 18

years according to a recent BNP Paribas report published on <u>Zero Hedge</u>; energy exporting emerging markets will be net importers of capital (by about $8bn) in 2014 due to reduced oil prices.

Interestingly, it was the Chinese who, in the wake of the 2008 crisis, revived talk of the Triffin Paradox. In a 2009 <u>speech</u> (hosted by the BIS no less), Dr. Zhou Xiaochuan, Governor of the People's Bank of China suggested:

> When a national currency is used in pricing primary commodities, trade settlements and is adopted as a reserve currency globally, efforts of the monetary authority issuing such a currency to address its economic imbalances by adjusting exchange rate would be made in vain, as its currency serves as a benchmark for many other currencies. While benefiting from a widely accepted reserve currency, the globalization also suffers from the flaws of such a system. The frequency and increasing intensity of financial crises following the collapse of the Bretton Woods system suggests the costs of such a system to the world may have exceeded its benefits. The price is becoming increasingly higher, not only for the users, but also for the issuers of the reserve currencies. Although crisis may not necessarily be an intended result of the issuing authorities, it is an inevitable outcome of the institutional flaws.

The SDR is Keynes' bancor arrived late.

As we venture into the shadow-world of unresolved dialectics (particularly those where resolution has been impudently asserted by one side) and the concomitant danger of allowing contradictions to fester beyond the moment history assigns for their timeliest resolution, one crystallizing moment suggests itself. The beginning of the end (as opposed to the end of the end) for the East-West struggle was implied at a <u>1992 diplomatic gathering</u> where a Pakistani Ambassador had the temerity to inquire of U.S. officials: "...you seem to believe that you won the Cold War, but did you ever consider the possibility that what has really happened is that the internal contradictions of communism caught up with communism before the internal contradictions of capitalism could catch up with capitalism?!"

This searing observation, in all likelihood ignored at the time, is perfectly apt for the present moment. The admonition to *know thyself*'s every bit as true for far-flung empires as it is for individuals, if not more so. Self-knowledge is a process, not a destination. Describing the 'universality of contradiction', Friedrich Engels noted that, "...a being is at each moment itself and yet something else." Because communism collapsed before capitalism, Russia was compelled to confront its many contradictions in a brutal, forthright manner. Time offered few luxuries. Armed with the benefit of hindsight, we might say history favored Russia by allowing its identity crisis to happen first. America's disadvantage was twofold: self-examination was deferred for additional decades and the Soviet Union's self-struggle furnished the necessary pretext for the US to claim a victory it hadn't really won. (Putin in his 2014 end-of-year press conference: "[the West] decided they were the winners, they were an empire, while all the others were their vassals, and they needed to put the squeeze on them.")

In terms of the Hegelian dialectic, Russia is arguably more spiritually realized than is the United States at this point in history. How interesting that the Russian Orthodox Church has enjoyed a coterminous renaissance during this period, wrought in no small part by suffering, all of which is good for the soul. Russia passed through the collectivist cauldrons of Bolshevism and democratic centralism, suffered, survived and prevailed. This legitimizes its progression to a further historic stage. America, by contrast, is only now venturing full bore into socialized medicine, a burgeoning internal security apparatus and command economy financial markets. Has it been paying any attention at all to history?

Grasping the essential interiority of the dialectical process (where one might say self-knowledge 'lives') Lenin traced what he called the 'kernel' of dialectics to, "the very essence of objects." Authentic struggle alters both combatants— deep down where it hurts. Yet American hubris could not countenance even that a dialectical process had been engaged, as admitting such robbed all savor from the imagined totality of the victory. (Already too perfect to alter a hair on his head, the narcissist refuses the dialectics of change and the inward mirror of introspection. America worships at the altar of winner-take-all: two teams, one winner. This binary oppositional frame readily accepts the Straussian Noble Lie of good versus evil. Of course the Rent Seeking Elite are themselves beyond good and evil.

Nonetheless the esotericists in their number paint a lurid, exoteric tale for mass consumption: WMD's, gruesome beheadings and the like. Dialectical resolution by contrast soils both combatants. Both thesis and antithesis relinquish their prior forms in the 'galvanizing events' that yield a synthesis.) America's cause was simply too just to countenance organic alteration as it prosecuted the Cold War with bullet-proof (and brittle) self-righteousness. The result, in the American mind at least, was that it won fair and square, and no further questions please.

PNAC can spout all the triumphalist blather it likes. (Frankly, the blood and lost treasure on that organization's hands are incalculable.) Not knowing what it had become, America barreled into one ruinous unipolar adventure after another. History however will not be cheated, nor will it be 'advanced ahead of itself'. We continue to see America's self-confusion manifesting in one strategic blunder after another: Libya, Syria, the Ukraine. Russia is too self-aware to be dragged back into recidivist dialectics settled years ago. Cold War II is for dummies. Russia has earned the right to move ahead. International Capital seems to understand this.

China is an historic curiosity for different reasons. The fuss over its economic ascendancy notwithstanding, there's that small matter of still being run by a centralized Communist Party. This is no mean anachronism. Jim Rickards has wryly noted that China is a political power often mistaken for an economic one. So, Russia has undergone extensive therapy. When will the other two superpowers catch up?

Dmitri Orlov offers hope that the Anglo-American Empire might yet avert war when he <u>suggests recently</u>: "There is still a chance to construct a new world order that will avoid a world war. This new world order must of necessity include the United States—but can only do so on the same terms as everyone else: subject to international law and international agreements; refraining from all unilateral action; in full respect of the sovereignty of other nations."

Orlov is always a compelling thinker, however this is a curious appeal indeed. For, what is the New World Order *other than* the ultimate extinguisher of national sovereignties? Nonetheless Orlov says, the US Empire must respect the sovereignty of its fellow nations so that, one supposes, a peaceful path can be cleared, allowing for the full-blown erasure of all national sovereignties at the hands of the New World Order. Furthermore, the "same terms as everyone else" are the unyielding terms of return on capital. Apparently Orlov would prefer that the New World Order do the extinguishing rather than the Anglo-American Empire. Frankly, Dmtri, does it matter? As for chance, nothing has been left to it. The New World Order is coming and it won't be stopped.

Reflecting on his 2014 trip to China last year as part of the Carter Center delegation, veteran Sinologist Orville Schell noted the increasing peremptoriness of Chinese officialdom to American power [underline added]:

> The Western presumption that China, aided by open markets, foreign education, and Western soft power, will irresistibly be swept toward ever greater political openness, which many

Westerners have come to view as the inevitable
(and desired) evolutionary path for every society,
is now being met by Chinese leaders with a loud
and defiant denial that could be summarized as
follows: <u>"We don't want to be in your teleological
dream!</u>
—from 'China Strikes Back!' by Orville Schell,
The New York Review of Books

The West's teleological dream, scripted (indeed coopted)
by International Capital, is mankind's shared nightmare.
After all, the road to *monos* is paved with one subsumed
civilization and empire after another. It risks Western
chauvinism, but China will suffer this fate too.

Of course the stubborn and deep-seated nationalist
sensibilities of China and Russia will militate against,
perhaps slightly delay, the inexorable upward consolidation
of International Capital. However, this too shall pass. Hive-
mind is destined to become humanity's discerning feature.
Usury's teleological dream will make it so. The efficient and
unimpeded flow of capital asks no less. God, country,
national sovereignty, ethnic pride represent topological
bumps on the flatland horizon demanded by monism.

The all-seeing eye of International Capitalism seeks a
perfect vista. Market transparency is one of its euphemistic
steamrollers. This sounds benign enough: *I'll show you mine if
you show me yours.* We hear it everywhere today, usually in a
reassuring way: Crooked banks must allow greater
transparency. Campaign finance reform is required in order
to bring transparency to the system. Yet as Political
Scientist Byung-Chul Han suggests, transparency hides a

darker lens [underline added]: "Things become transparent when they divest their singularity and express themselves entirely through price. Money, which allows everything to be compared to everything else, completely eliminates the incommensurability and singularity of things. Transparency society is a <u>hell of sameness</u>."—from '<u>Transparency Society</u>', by Byung-Chul Han

Transparency is its own form of blindness. Taking a more figurative interpretive approach, Islamic eschatologist Sheikh Imran Hosein <u>suggests</u> the One eye bespeaks a malady caused by the eye of the heart being closed. Thus the one-eyed *Dajjal* spoken of in the Quran may be less anatomical description as systemic feature. One wonders how the opaque nature of Chinese power will reconcile against the transparency prerogatives of International Capital.

So, International Capital has already passed *through* the Anglo-American empire on the way to more capital-friendly locales, namely China and Russia, the latter two far better situated—both temperamentally, geographically, fiscally and synergistically—to exploit a Eurasian Century which belongs in no small part to the IMF as well. Here again though, the danger lies in over-interpolating the East-West dialectic in a manner that suggests both nations are in sudden lockstep. In his 2014 end of year press conference, Putin himself helped deflate the east-west pivot-talk in very explicit pipeline terms, saying [underline added]:

> In addition, [the China gas deal] will help Russia, which will receive and accumulate gigantic resources at the project's initial stage, to begin

connecting our Far Eastern regions to the gas distribution grids, not just to export gas through the pipeline. This will allow us to make the next – a very important – step. <u>We will be able to link together the western and eastern gas pipeline systems and promptly re-channel resources back and forth when needed,</u> depending on the international market. This is very important. Without it, we would never be able to connect Eastern Siberia and the Far East to the gas distribution system.

Of course, the America China faces is not the belligerent existential threat that bedevils Russia. Herein lies the material for continued triangulation though perhaps with China in a more assertive role. Yes, China has been unequivocal in its support of the ruble in the wake of Western sanctions. However, this support is born of triangulating self-interest, with no accompanying chill manifesting towards the US. Just last month at the annual China-US Joint Commission on Commerce and Trade (JCCT), <u>China Daily</u> quotes Chinese Vice Premier Wang Yang:

> "This JCCT session added a perfect finishing touch to this year's development of China-US relations, and also laid a solid foundation for our bilateral economic and trade cooperation next year and in the long run," Wang, who arrived in Chicago Tuesday, told the American hosts during their initial talks.

He also expressed the belief that China and the United States have much more common interests than differences, and that their economic and trade cooperation will prosper as long as the two countries can "seek common ground while reserving differences" in the spirit of mutual respect, mutual understanding and mutual accommodation.

Sources with the Chinese delegation told Xinhua that during the session, the US side also repeatedly emphasized the significance of US-China cooperation for both economies and the world economy at large, and expressed its readiness to work with the Chinese side on the basis of mutual respect and mutual benefit to lift economic and trade ties to a new height."

Nonetheless the prospect of substantive rapprochement between Russia and China is what keeps the Brzezinski's of the world awake at night. There is much in the way of historical antagonisms to be overcome. Yet the synergies, as a recent <u>White Paper</u> (from a purported China insider) at the Vineyard of the Saker blog suggests, are deeply compelling. Time will tell.

Someday, the globalists dream, the weight of empire will resemble, in hindsight, an onerous and provincial endeavor, clumsily *de rigueur*—something International Capital will be gladly rid of, and good riddance! The socio-political Panopticon that follows after monetary union will have no further need of dialectical kabuki theater nor the goofy calisthenics of managed opposition. Those games will belong to a fractious bygone era. The days of politically coerced (or militarily acquired) empire are over, not because global ambitions have abated; rather, because geopolitical hegemony will arrive, globally scaled, on the heels of monetary hegemony. Just as the road to world government runs through the BIS and IMF, the day will soon arrive when empires are replaced with regional zones of influence. Nations will be shadows of their former selves, atrophying into administrative districts.

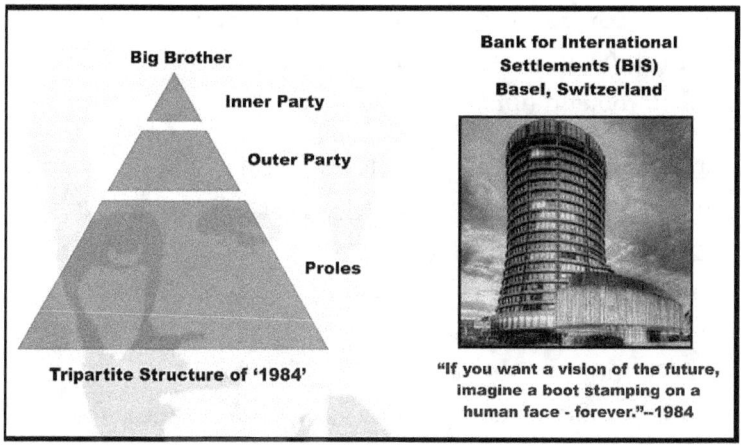

Big Brother
Inner Party
Outer Party
Proles
Tripartite Structure of '1984'

Bank for International Settlements (BIS) Basel, Switzerland

"If you want a vision of the future, imagine a boot stamping on a human face - forever."--1984

No less than Zbigniew Brzezinski has conceded the impracticality of old-school Empire on a politically awakened planet. Pax Americana, a most thoroughly useful engine, made the world safe for dollar impregnation, *allowing everything to be compared with everything else* (Byung-Chul Han). The manifold is continually narrowing its feature list to better accommodate the reductionist ethos of the *monos*. Dollarization was a crucial normalization phase on the way to perfect control. Today, everyone is on the same foundering page. The world—and its beleaguered currencies—are poised to 'swoon upwards' into the arms of the IMF. How the Anglo-American Empire differs from its predecessors is that its abundantly advertised grotesqueries will be used by International Capital to disabuse the world of nationalist excesses. 'Never again' will be the mantra. The IMF and BIS will rise to the fore on the pledge that multi-polarity must prevail forevermore. Of course the latter arrangement will dilute sovereignty and strengthen the mandate for a world government. We are being conducted (in brave new world fashion) towards a seamless ubiquity with flattened differentiators, non-assertive control and a global village mono-culture. The American Century is dead. Empire itself is dead. Long live the IMF millennium.

Martin Armstrong is practically alone among market analysts in <u>seeing the political sphere morphing into a gestapo-like collections agency</u>, both for itself (the Rent Seeking Elite) and for International Capital: "When I say there is a worldwide hunt for capital that is destroying the world economy – this is NO JOKE! Politicians have spent whatever they like and then imprison citizens for not handing over whatever they demand. This is not democracy – it is totalitarianism…Government has abused its power and looks upon the people as a herd of unwashed wild animals for them to drive in whatever direction they desire for their own self-interest."

The Rent Seeking Elites are becoming more unabashedly extractive as Capital insists on debt service before growth. Slowly, the People slip beneath a fascistic boot (More than one commentator has pointed out the BIS headquarters in Basel's eerie resemblance to an Orwellian jackboot.) However is Armstrong's inference misdirected? Perhaps the 'hunt for capital' is nothing less than capital gathering itself back up in a final reconsolidation phase; the destruction of the world economy not so much a horrible effect wrought by a short-sighted Rent Seeking Elite as an intended end dictated by International Capital. Capital and the People are parties to the same narrative, but from entirely different vantages.

Part Three: The Currency Reset and Beyond

"We've achieved a level of tangible, global economic cooperation that we've never seen before. Our financial system will be far different and more secure than the one that failed so dramatically last year."

—from President Barak Obama, G20 Meeting, 2009

In the first two parts of this series, we looked at the indispensable role of usury in the consolidation of monetary power on Earth and the class system employed to bring this consolidation about. Then we went on to explore the transient or vehicular role empires play within International Capital's scheme and the inevitable currency debasements that ensue. This final part of the series speculates on the final currency hand-off from the presiding US Dollar (the last empire) to an international one-world currency, the IMF's Special Drawing Rights or SDR.

Funny things happen on the way to the forum. Laggards arrive first. Leaders get lost. Empire is not a birthright. International Capital tolerates the inevitable corruption of its Rent Seeking Elites, recognizing it as a cost of doing business. However in time, Empire becomes a myopic cocoon so riven with corruption that even International Capital abandons it to its decadence. Wall Street has long since ceased its capital intermediation functions for brazen and systemic corruption. International Capital perceives the ebbing value of the Wall Street elite. All Rent Seeking Elites are corrupt. However it is a matter of workable degree. The

Anglo-American elite is at such an apogee (nadir?) of corruption that its can no longer sustain even the illusion prescribed by the rule of law. Contempt is growing amongst the masses. This is a fatal mistake as International Capital is loyal only to itself. In the final act, the Rent Seeking Elite are universally despised.

Though hardly paragons of virtue, Russia and China don't need to be told that industrial production and infrastructure development are more than rationalizing platforms for financialized rent-seeking. That's a lecture more befitting the decadent West. China builds silk roads and railways. Russia excels at large infrastructure projects, weapons technology and harbors abundant resources; while American Empire has been reduced to building sanction-coalitions and enforcing promissory notes. How grim having to charge around the world, light on industrial capacity, heavy on guns, shouting: 'Use my currency or I'll shoot!' In a world parched for growth (or if you prefer, choked with debt) American Empire has become obstructionist and cranky. These are contractive, not expansive behaviors. Bankers hate deflation. For them, it's the Sisyphean boulder rolled down the hill. Debt service requires an ever-higher altitude. Onwards and upwards!

So how smoothly will this monetary reset proceed? Much depends on where one sits on the seesaw. The US' predicament is particularly precarious, and not simply because of the size of its debt. To understand this, it's important to realize that the currency reset in some ways is catching up to a 'creeping power reset' which has been decades in the making, and which will further extend its consolidation aided by the SDR as world reserve currency.

The FOFOA blog attempts to describe the morning-after impact of this unprecedented global currency reset in matrix terms (though the full transition will extend at least through 2018):

> This transfer of wealth that is coming is not a direct and equal transfer. It is not like pouring one pitcher into another. It is more like flipping a switch on the virtual matrix. Turning off the monetary plane that hovers over the physical plane and claims to tell you how much "stored purchasing power" everyone has. When you turn it off, all that purchasing power disappears in a flash. And then what lies beneath is exposed in daylight, the real physical world. No real capital is destroyed, only the myth is destroyed. But true capital is exposed and revalued.

A crisis in value is always a crisis in values. Those who know themselves well will fare best. Those who calibrate themselves mostly by what they *have* will founder. Adding to the confusion is a sense of complacency in the West resulting from decades absent a currency collapse. Indeed western societies' faith in paper amazes more volatile regions of the world. The USD is not an impregnable storehouse of value. Such belief, FOFOA Blog insists, is badly misplaced:

> One should grasp that "today, your wealth, is not what your currency says it is"! In this world, paper currency is for trade, only! It is for the buying, selling, earning and paying, not for knowing the value of your family holdings! Know this, "the

printers of paper do never tell the owner that the
money has less value, that judgment is reserved
for the person you offer that currency to".

Suffice to say many will be distraught at the meagerness of
their reset allotment.

The global currency reset will be an early thrust in a much
broader repositioning of International Capital's 21ˢᵗ century
attentions. Reset losers will fast recede into yesterday's
news as the decks are rearranged to optimize an assault on
what journalist Pepe Escobar has long called the looming
and resplendent <u>Eurasian Century</u>. From his coining of the
Empire of Chaos epithet to his boots-on-the-ground
reportage, Escobar has been out front insisting Anglo-
America is not the Empire to mount this assault. He
captures the essence of the east-west horizontal struggle
here: "At present, the choice between the two available
models on the planet seems stark indeed: Eurasian
integration or a spreading empire of chaos." Whether he
acknowledges the puppet-master astride this dialectic is less
clear.

Much of the tension we see today arises from Rent Seeking
Elites of various nations jostling for pecking order within
the imminent new global "monetary plane". The IMF SDR
currency reset lies perhaps mere weeks away.
Understanding there's a switch on the wall and a hand
moving steadily towards it helps clarify the game.

The Philosophy of Metrics blog <u>furnishes one more
tantalizing clue</u> (below) towards understanding the rationale
behind the sanctions campaign against Russia. China's
recent <u>ruble swaps</u> may be, among other things, a

countermeasure aimed at boosting Russia's SDR prospects (and reducing the American component). That sounds like clever triangulation. Is the Ukraine ground zero for the first Currency Basket War?

> One matter of interest in the 2010 [IMF] Reforms is the restoration of Russian representation and quota shares, which would see an increase for the resource rich country back to 2.71% from 2.49%. Though this may appear inconsequential on the surface, when we consider that the Russian ruble was the 18th most used currency in the world, (as of September, 2014) out of 150 currencies in the world, and that demand has increased for the ruble to act as a regional reserve currency throughout Eastern Europe, Central Asia, and the Caucasus, the geopolitical strategies playing out in Ukraine become much clearer.

Most likely, the ensuing currency rebalancing and debt reallocations will cause disruptions of decades-long living standards, especially in the US. Domestic social unrest is all but assured. The recent decline in oil prices and the movement of gold inventories between nations no doubt contain elements of SDR strategic positioning and rebalancing as well.

As though cued to this currency reset, a recent spate of fast-moving developments suggest American Empire is being readied for yet another wave of global opprobrium. These include:

- Senator Barbara Feinstein's shocking report on CIA torture abuse.

- Dick Cheney's increasingly frigid turns on TV (*et tu* Fox News?!) as the Bush Administration's not-so congenial apologist for rectal rehydration.
- The New York Times' blistering '<u>Prosecute Torturers and Their Bosses</u>' editorial.
- Seymour Hersh's <u>hints</u> that even more heinous Abu Ghraib torture practices will soon be laid bare.

A lead-in narrative of failed moral leadership portends larger troubles ahead. Lyndon Larouche was emboldened enough recently to trumpet the arrival of the 'post-911' era, his optimism leavened somewhat by the escalating threat of thermonuclear war. This post-911 era, should it arrive absent a nuclear winter, signals nothing less than the passing of the baton *upwards* from the planet's last Empire to what will be touted as a more stable multipolar world:

> What the Feinstein revelations on CIA torture portend, is the end of the entire post-9/11 dynamic, which the United States—for the entire 14 years of this 21st Century, under two Bush administrations and two Obama administrations—has been marshaled by the British Empire as an aggressive imperial force, up to and including threatening thermonuclear war against Russia and China today.—from the <u>December 19, 2014 issue</u> of Executive Intelligence Review.

On the economic front, the Anglo-American Empire is proving an abysmal global steward in two crucial areas. These discontents could easily be sharpened as part of an

'America as global pariah' narrative. First, Congress' failure to ratify the 2010 IMF reforms presents a huge uncertainty as the world enters the New Year, when currency markets are jittery enough already. The beggar thy neighbor currency war climate is fostering 'fiat anxiety' the world over. A fresh paper regime will find it hard enough overcoming popular skepticism without having to climb an even steeper wall of worry. Finally, the drama queen act by the IMF's most favored nation as it pulls a pariah state impersonation at the 11th hour only furthers the notion that the US should be stripped of the parental right of IMF veto. In short, the US is making an excellent case for its own diminished role. One must wonder, has this lurid display of self-destruction been prescribed in advance? The degree of intentionality is always a matter of debate.

The more contentious the SDR transition, the greater a role gold will play, either in percentage terms as a SDR basket component or as some kind of alternative in the event of SDR adoption failure. IMF Chairwoman Christine Lagarde has a Plan B in the event of continued American intransigence that almost certainly dilutes US influence. Edwin Truman suggests US risks and costs are negligible for Plan A approval. Why then does America dither? Perhaps there is a larger directed narrative at play— Brandon Smith opts for the larger conspiracy trope when he suggests:

> [T]he strategy [is for] international financiers to create a dollar-collapse scenario that will be blamed on prepositioned scapegoats. I have no idea what form these scapegoats will take - there are simply too many possible triggers for fiscal

calamity. What I do know, though, is the goal of the endgame: to remove the dollar's world reserve status and to pressure the American people into conforming or even begging for centralized administration of our economy by the IMF.

Smith is right. How exactly the wheels come off the train is not as important as that they will come off. *Monos* assures gravity always moves up. A derivatives collapse in the wake of the 50% decline in oil prices would serve nicely (especially as all FDIC-insured deposits are now on the hook for evisceration, thanks to the recent repeal of a key Dodd-Frank rule.) Ellen Brown, renowned author of Web of Debt <u>predicts</u> that, after the derivatives collapse, "little banks will go out of business, and who is going to survive— the big banks…What we're going to have left is five big banks, and everybody else is going to be bankrupt." The pyramid narrows yet again. We are led to believe Wall Street is careening forward blind with greed. Of course, this is true. What's less understood however is how International Capital plans to advantage this greed in order to, in effect, pivot beyond it on the way to Eurasia's greener pastures. Horizontal dialectics serve vertical consolidation. The *monos* always wins.

The USD is designed to fall just short of the globalist mission, 'failing up' into the arms of the IMF. That's why the capstone floats, disembodied, atop the Dollar Bill pyramid. No mere empire will consolidate International Capital's triumphant project. *Pax Americana* leaves unfinished business behind. Smith also offers the most plausible account of the <u>buyer of $340 billion in USD Treasury Bonds</u> in recent months (third behind only China and Japan) being not Belgium, the official buyer, but an IMF/BIS proxy. This debt will be used as a bargaining chip in the austerity measures almost certain to be imposed on the US, post-collapse. America's exorbitant privilege is about to come due in the manner of a massive and crippling debt restructuring.

Empires are factionalized and complex, especially at points of inflection. The elite can be of many minds. There's a strong likelihood all is not well in the kingdom. Treasury Secretary Jack Lew represents the IMF faction within the Obama Administration. The Republican Congress is playing obstructionist on IMF reforms for reasons that aren't clear. For her part, Lagarde sounds genuinely upset. One would think she should be. The IMF's credibility in the eyes of the world is at stake. Why author a script that invokes institutional self-humiliation if the IMF is poised to assume a more active global presence?

> "The IMF's membership has been calling on and was expecting the United States to approve the IMF's 2010 Quota and Governance Reforms by year end," Lagarde said in a statement.
>
> "Adoption of the reforms remains critical to strengthening the Fund's credibility, legitimacy, and effectiveness, and to ensure it has sufficient permanent resources to meet its members' needs. I have expressed my disappointment to the US authorities and hope that they continue to work toward speedy ratification.—from 'IMF's Lagarde 'Disappointed' by US Inaction on Reforms' , Yahoo News, December 12, 2014

The most successful gold-bugs are gold dealers. Gold hoarders are like the guy who buys an expensive home insurance policy only to fly into a rage every day his house doesn't burn down. That said, every stopped clock gets a couple of heroic moments. Jim Rickards has a backstop scenario lined up for us in 'Currency Wars' and yes, it involves our favorite shining consternation: "When all else fails, possibly including a new SDR plan, gold is always waiting in the wings as a stable, widely accepted store of value and universal money. In the end, a global struggle between gold and SDRs for supremacy as "money" may be the next great shock added to the long list of historic shocks to the international monetary system."

The second major demerit against the US as a responsible steward of the world economy has to do with the Fed's Quantitative Easing x.0 and Zero Interest Rate Policy (ZIRP). Intended to jump-start the domestic economy, this free money orgy suddenly remembered there was a big world out there to shake down. So it overflowed into the emerging markets to the tune of $5.7 trillion. That's a lot of overflow: "…the 'emerging governments' borrowed those cheap US dollars using anything not bolted down, including their national treasures, as collateral, and they now face a doubling, tripling, quadrupling etc. of the interest rates they have to pay on those loans."—from 'The Fed Kills Emerging Markets For Profit", Zero Hedge, 9/23/2014

There's a great NWO pick-up line lurking thereabouts as the world picks itself up in the aftermath of deflationary collapse. Rest assured, the ghost of Triffin will inhabit

Lagarde's 2016 victory speech: *Never again shall a national currency be allowed to hold such devastating sway over the world economy!* [Applause from the impoverished sheeple.] We will sprint into the arms of our captors. In this regard Huxley trumps Orwell. The perfect system will be consensual not coercive. The very need for force is a sign perfection still eludes and that manufactured consent has unfinished business.

Empires are episodic way-stations created to serve Capital's interests. The delusional machinations of hubris can have elites mistaking guest turns for enduring birthrights. During this critical migration of International Capital's affections, thermonuclear tantrum or ill-judged military industrial accident from a jilted elite cannot be ruled out. This would be the last desperate gasp of a fading hegemon, a frightening enough prospect perhaps to compel International Capital out of its preferred Darwinian mode and into a more activist and supervisory role. No group of human beings can possibly want widespread nuclear devastation.

The modern consciousness is trained on Hollywood conspiracy scripts where the most intricate plots cleverly resolve themselves in the final minutes. Attending this expectation is the notion that the Evil Elite have everything in hand. Much more likely, there is trepidation at the highest reaches of power. The risks of a global reset and the potential for unforeseen consequences are high. Life imitates art as conspiracy aficionados routinely get away with murder in their rearguard attempts to maintain plot consistency. When things don't quite pan out, the staples of the paranoid are 'PsyOps', 'disinformation' and 'controlled chaos'. However, there's nothing controlled about thermonuclear war except in the most deranged minds. Unscripted madness may well lurk somewhere in the mix. The numbers are simply too large, the immense power too long enjoyed that a desperate rogue action cannot be ruled out. Let's hope not.

Joel Skousen remains convinced that, from the ashes of MAD, a first-strike phoenix will rise just as America's elite repairs to well-appointed underground bunkers. They will re-emerge onto a landscape devastated by Chinese and Russian counterstrike. But they will be, once again, in control of all the rubble they survey. The dazed remnants of America will rally around its recently re-surfaced, scandalously complicit saviors. No one will think to bring up such ornamental concerns as civil rights and Internet freedoms—not after what just happened! There are even suggestions International Capital itself seeks a thermonuclear 'galvanizing event' in order to secure savior status for itself and win popular consent for a world government. These 'soil your own nest with Cesium-137' conspiracies that are ascribed to people who *already* own the world simply fail, in this writer's opinion, the credulity test.

There's always the proverbial third way—restoring the USD to sovereign (government-issued) currency status with a staged transition away from the Federal Reserve Note. Alas, the two most likely currency alternatives are varying degrees of more-of-the-same: a continuation of the USD as debt-money world reserve currency (i.e. a mere postponement of inevitable Ponzi collapse) or transition to the SDR (i.e. swapping a Ponzi for a bigger Ponzi) on the way to the NWO.

If International Capital ever allowed reintroduction of a sovereign US currency, it would be a sure sign the former is radically diverting its attentions, a gut-wrenching prospect no matter how one feels about the bankers. Monetary systems are not constructed overnight. Damon Vrabel has speculated the recent prevalence of the 'End the Fed' meme in mainstream media outlets might suggest such an anticipated departure. International Capital would be acceding to Ron Paul's demand, in effect saying, 'so you want to close the teller window? Fine.' Clearly, Capital's future lies in Asia where America's production capacity has already been moved. Meanwhile, America's key 'contribution' to the world economy, consumer demand, is unsustainable without reserve currency status, and easily supplanted by emerging consumer markets abroad. So much for the value chain. It doesn't take a genius to buy stuff. The American Liberty movement needs to ask itself, in the absence of the Fed how the US would access capital. And please, the gold standard is a deflationary dead duck.

American exceptionalism can hardly imagine a world that it does not sit astride let alone one that precludes it from substantive participation altogether. Brandon Smith's imaginings along these lines represent the absolute worst case scenario, one in which America slides from first to third world status, practically in the flash of a keystroke. Almost certainly, 2015 is the year such a flush will happen:

> Imagine what would happen if all foreign creditors abandoned U.S. debt purchases because

the dollar was no longer seen as viable as a world reserve currency. Imagine that the Fed's efforts to stimulate through fiat printing became useless in propping up Treasuries, serving only to devalue the domestic buying power of our currency. Imagine that the IMF swoops in as the lender of last resort; the only entity willing to service our debt and keep the system running. Imagine what kind of concessions America would have to make to a global loan shark like the IMF.

If there is a spokesman for International Capital, then surely it is the Bank of International Settlements (BIS), often referred to as the Central Bankers' Bank. When the BIS expresses puzzlement and concern, as it last did in 2008, trouble is either brewing or being made to look so. Here it is, sounding notes of *déjà vu* all over again:

> "A long-standing puzzle in international finance is the durability of the dollar's share of foreign exchange reserves - which remains above 60%, while the weight of the US economy in global output has fallen to less than a quarter."

> "The appreciation of the dollar against the backdrop of divergent monetary policies may, if persistent, have a profound impact on the global economy, in particular on EMEs...A continued depreciation of the domestic currency against the dollar could reduce the creditworthiness of many firms, potentially inducing a tightening of financial conditions."

—from <u>BIS Quarterly Review, December, 2014</u>

Any Empire that finds itself simultaneously on the wrong side of the IMF, the BIS, the BRICS nations and normal standards of human decency (war crimes anyone?) is working hard at losing the designation. In fact the US is looking so bad on so many fronts, all at the same time that one could be forgiven for suspecting a big wind-up in advance of a big wind-down. Is QE/ZIRP a plan to lure the entire world into a USD *cul de sac*? Borrowing in another nation's currency is like walking into a jail cell to await the click of the key. The only balance sheet big enough to kiss away the world's boo-boos will be the IMF's. Even now, the USD is sucking the air out of the entire planet with one last violent spasm of appreciation. There is a massive USD short squeeze underway.

This would mean Lagarde and the BIS are openly wringing their hands in telegraphed dismay. (Remember, the BIS *is* the Fed to some extent as the latter is a board member of the former. Who directs whom is harder to glean.) This 'Blame the Fed' narrative seems bound to crescendo in early-mid 2015.

Meanwhile, the Philosophy of Metrics <u>blog</u> asks—in the specific context here of Republican Party motives—just how much of what we see is a '*plan* to create a situation' versus 'a *game* fraught with randomness'?

> Do the Republicans have the political capital and international influence to continue holding the world ransom? Highly unlikely. And if they do continue to delay then we can assume that the

plan is to create a situation where the US
influence and dollar are removed from the IMF
under the umbrella of a *de-facto* financial
coup…the game being played is intriguing and
fraught with increasing chances of randomness.

Given their abdication on the IMF 2010 reforms, one
wonders what the Republican Party is thinking. (Listening
to John Boehner on any number of topics, it's easy to say
'not a whole lot'.) Are we over-interpolating a plan in the
face of randomized inertia? There seems little advantage to
the GOP antagonizing the IMF *unless of course it's supposed to*
(or has been bribed to; China perhaps seeking delay for
reasons unknown.)

There's a tendency in the conspiracy narratives to have it
both ways. Either there's an inordinate number of
sociopaths at the highest reaches of power or there's this
interpersonally 'harmonious' oblong table around which the
Grand Conspirators strategize, complete with a recognized
pecking order. Assigning subtasks to megalomaniacs could
make herding cats the stuff of child's play. Convergent
interests can be a powerful force that functionally
approximates explicit conspiracy. International Capital is
not in need of an oblong table. In the end though, does it
really matter, since the effect is the same?

The fault dear Brutus may lie not as much in *their*
Impeccably Diabolical Plan as in *our* need to exculpate
personal responsibility by over-inferring their supreme
mastery. Freud would call it determined transference. After
all, Capital loans to avarice and greed. Our character flaws
and failings permeate the deepest darkest conspiracy

narratives. The conspiratorial mind excels at seeing a plan, even in random events. This is a cognitive predilection that often reveals more about the observer than the observed. The danger lies is succumbing to self-negating, Prison Planet paranoia. Even with a plan, the roles of the players are not always as they appear. Tactically too, a plan of such consummating ambition no doubt adjusts with some frequency. The larger point is that this infernal force called usury has an intentionality unto itself. So perhaps sweating the details as to the level of certain men's foreknowledge is a pointless exercise.

Though tightly-woven conspiracy narratives may indulge a too-close reading of events, the purposeful arc of history is not so easily repealed. International Capital is destroying *our* vision on the way to a more perfected realization of *its* vision. Though these competing visions are antithetical, an unexamined parallelism was encouraged to prevail. Our belief in a better life traveled with their unassailable knowledge that life belonged in the end only to them. This contradiction will be sustained until it is no longer tenable.

Our chaste belief that something lay ahead for all of us (if we would only let this machine impose its regimen of 'efficiencies and transparencies' across the globe) was a tragic misread. The middle class, with its notions of upward mobility and enduring prosperity, was the grandest, cruelest daydream of all.

Part of this machine's teleological advancement involved creating an aspirant class in the midterm. The evaporating middle class is like a wake in the midst of a long sea voyage. The wake, in its fervor, can be forgiven for thinking it was the reason the boat sped across the water. In fact the captain had much more on his mind. He was in a hurry to reach the other side where he knew the wake would subside once the destination was reached. Some of the disturbed waters, the captain knew, would break across the shore (the occasional poet, the occasion fool). But these were minor inundations that would soon expend their energies and be done.

In order to get it arms around the earth, International Capital had to entice broad swathes of people with the veritable crumbs of prosperity. Capital thus allowed capitalism, though no doubt with reservations. There was a risk to raising mass expectations. However manufactured consent paired with money supply control has proven quite effective in managing expectations up, then ever so carefully back down. Economist Henry C. K. Liu's quote bears repeating here: "Reversing the logic that a sound banking system should lead to full employment and developmental growth, BIS regulations demand high unemployment and developmental degradation in national economies as the fair price for a sound global private banking system."

In fact the logic was never reversed. We drew our own logic with a wishfulness that a clear understanding of the system never justified. Full employment? That sounds like everybody eating. Capital is loath to acknowledge subsistence wages. When has it ever pursued full bellies for all?

We were encouraged in that false historic read as it made us ever more diligent carriers of the usury virus. The system encouraged the fanning of our expectations. Now prosperity is being repealed. He who owns the gold narrates the final chapter. A good-faith accommodation was never struck between Labor and Capital. Capital made no concessions it did not intend one day to take back. Global deflation marks the rescission of inflated expectations. As a bridge to true wealth, loan activity was always a mirage. Wealth is returning to where it only ever pretended to depart. Above our heads. Beyond our reach. Like all loans, the terms always favored the lender. Capital doesn't share. The *monos* seeks its own company. Men pledged to capital are not men at all. They are gilded cogs. Soul escapes the machine to reside at the bottom, where the suffering is greatest, where the humanity is least challenged.

This essay has attempted to suggest an eschatological consolidation is afoot, and in a manner that avoids accusations of gratuitous pattern-seeking and the worst of montaged *Youtube* Illuminati-izing. We all must contend with the directedness versus randomness conundrum: what to leave in, what to leave out. May good sense allow us to see Henry Kissinger peering from behind a bush only when he's really there.

International Capital insists on the forced march of upward consolidation towards an altitude where, it will be shown, no man can breathe. Indeed even those today sitting astride this 'rough beast whose time has come' daydream atop a human threshing machine. The apotheosis of the Beast is the cessation of all human impulse. Mammon, in the final act, will not countenance even a human figurehead sitting astride his Babelian tower. Hell on earth will commence when the Antichrist relinquishes his last vestige of humanity, becoming the Devil Incarnate. Truly those will be the worst, last days on earth.

In an earlier phase, International Capital was content to curtail man through the subsistence wage necessitated by capitalism's central crisis, overproduction. Today, man's labor is extraneous at any price as he finds himself excised from the equation altogether. The pyramid walls narrow yet again. Capital is the endless recycled labor of dead men risen anew in one debt obligation after another to visit exploitation on their children and children's children. What is a pyramid after all but a tomb commemorating the dead?

Even transhumanist Hugo de Garis is sanguine on mankind's prospects in a world 'peopled' by Artilects. Just as *monos* is the apotheosis of nihilism, trans-humanism heralds the arrival of post-humanism. The ineluctable and inhuman gears of usury will deliver the world to machines of even more fabulous capacity. Our imprimatur will vanish from the face of the Earth. Therein lies the nasty surprise of usury's final bestowal: No man will live to receive it.

Unless a radically exogenous intervention ensues, there is no power on earth capable of arresting the quickening and diabolical *telos* of *e pluribus monos*. Only Christ can undo all that usury has wrought.

Where are the churches?

When Currency Becomes a Fiat for Oxygen, All Breathing Must Leave the Room

"This business about appetite for risk or ability to shift risk is all crap."-- from The Institutional Risk Analyst, 2008

(originally appeared in iTulip and <u>The Potomac Journal,</u> circa early 2009)

[Author's note: Here is another circa late 2008 essay that still encapsulates much of what is currently transpiring.]

SOMETHING IS AFOOT THAT, SO FAR, eludes the most sprawling macro-economic theories. Like the ultimate exogeneity or game-changing black swan, the best evidence of a dawning paradigm is that few things make sense through the old glasses. As T. S. Eliot remarked of great poetry (and I paraphrase), its arrival is felt before its impact is understood. In this instance, we will regret mistaking a lack of understanding for a lack of arrival.

Not surprisingly, all roads lead to modern-day Rome. Indeed there is a super-dimensional aspect to America's most-favored nation status as propagator of the world's reserve currency. When Zimbabwe prints money, hyper-inflation results, the standard textbook stuff. Land reform programs (i.e. taking arable land from those with green thumbs and giving it to those with brown noses) will earn you 11,000,000% inflation or greater.

It's said the rich are different. So is King Dollar. Indeed Mugabe must salivate at American alchemy as Fed Chairman Ben Bernanke's profligacy spurs a 'flight to dollar safety'. It doesn't take a PhD in Economics to glean that business as usual has been shattered. Fed panic speaks in the sheer verticality. The recent growth in the US monetary base has been nothing short of parabolic. It seems the Fed has been shooting a fire-hose through a pin-hole --the pin-hole being the banking industry's reluctance to create fresh loan activity from torrents of new money as they preoccupy themselves with rebuilding capital reserves. Basic economics tell us that, while inflation can be postponed, it cannot permanently be repealed. Not with repeated helicopter drops like this. The ghost is in the machine. Now we await its apparition.

America should take little comfort from its currency's relative strength. However one calibrates the chutes and ladders, the dollar, once proud eagle, has become a pigeon among sparrows. But shock of shocks, the dollar is strengthening. Indeed there may be a technical (read: temporary) complexion to the recent dollar run-up. (See Confusion reigns: A crisis-driven global rush to dollar liquidity is not deflation.) As the world shifts, panic-stricken, from one troubled asset class to the next, each swoon must pass through the dollar toll-booth. Thus we find wholesale panic bullish for the reserve currency. As Jesse's Café Americain October 2 blog entry describes, European current demand for dollars is acute but really a short-term artificiality caused by "a currency imbalance [that] increases the cost of euro-dollar swaps". (See this link for more info).

Thus the last few weeks' event of a strengthening dollar – *vis a vis* practically everything else – only mimics the trend of deflation. As Jesse says elsewhere, in the midst of "a short term liquidity crunch, traders, in this case most likely hedge funds and small speculators, go into panic selling to address margin calls and short term cash obligations."

69

Deflation would require a conscious central bank policy to raise interest rates, not likely. Dollar strength is thus an unsustainable aberration. Inflation is all but assured.

America should take little comfort from its currency's relative strength. However one calibrates the chutes and ladders, the dollar, once proud eagle, has become a pigeon among sparrows. Moreover the diminishment is a global phenomenon. No boat can avert a receding tide. The world's economy will emerge from this debacle economy-sized. Isn't it a bit supercilious then to crow that the highest man clinging to the mast of a sinking ship is in a position of 'relative safety' when the ship, the currency complex, is sinking? So the last man drowns last. Big deal.

Beyond even these technical machinations, there is a ghost in the machinery of the currency complex that betrays a measure of irrationality, a non-quantifiable 'fealty' to dollars. Call it a force of habit. Other apt analogies? The Divine Right of Kings, Pax Romana. People are swimming – partly as an act of faith, partly from a half-century of ingrained habit – towards a lifeboat with a fatal leak. What's the alternative, hugging a wave? For those who prefer casting aspersions with their last breath, they might shout, who didn't pack a second lifeboat? Perhaps it's not a lifeboat at all that will save us, but an island – gold. Perhaps there are better, more utilitarian, stores of intrinsic value: cigarettes, nylons and chocolate for example. Own a warehouse of ciggies and you may one day preside over a small mid-western town. (See Negative "Positive Feedback Loop" of Employment and Housing.)

The bitter prospect of marking-to-market is an admission of lost might, a medicine far too hard to swallow. Though wealth can evaporate overnight, belief systems tend to linger beyond their period of efficacy. A belief system that has held sway for the better part of a half-century, Pax Americana, is bankrupt (literally), and risking hyper-inflation (after perhaps a brief deflationary interlude) as it strives mightily to forestall the inexorable process of its decline. History is littered with denialists (See iTulip Ka-Poom Theory, 1999). The bitter prospect of marking-to-market is an admission of lost might, a medicine far too hard to swallow. An empire collapses back to more manageable perimeters only with great reluctance. For one thing, retreat precipitates ugly feed-back loops. Other uppity frontier regions become emboldened. The empire buzzes with insurrection. The powers-that-be will embrace denial before they embrace retreat. We are about to learn just how dangerous a wounded Master of the Universe can be.

Jaw-Boning

Depression. That's a word they're loath to say,
the men whose jobs revolve around the myth
that words, like sticks and stones, put trends in play
not easily reversed. They'll take the fifth
before reciting populist accounts
as though hard times held under house arrest
might huddle in the basement. All that counts
is what gets counted --keep the bloody rest.
No gesture pays for braces. No harangue
can cure the blind of pathologic greed.
Econometric models lack the pang
of hunger. How the poor excel at need.
Depression means no money, simply put
--a truth too bare to snare a tailored suit.
--*Norman Ball*

How can the world purge itself of dollars when it is awash in them? It pays to remember currencies are comparative, not intrinsic, stores of value. Thus purging oneself of a currency always involves bingeing on another. One wonders, can the Pax Americana/Bretton Woods/Plaza Accord regime truly hand the baton to a new world order (lower case) without a resounding capitulation followed by an ensuing period of collapse? The Visigoths destroyed Rome. Centuries of darkness ensued before Pax Britannia re-ordered the world. But take solace, my broadband brethren. In the digital era, the prior business of centuries now concludes itself in mere decades if not years. Computers aren't going away.

How can the world purge itself of dollars when it is awash in them? It pays to remember currencies are comparative, not intrinsic, stores of value. Thus purging oneself of a currency always involves bingeing on another. In an era of dwindling resources and looming peak oil, resource proxies are looking good – gold, oil. The euro might have served nicely as an orderly re-assembly point. But it's hard to imagine the long-term twin collapse of the dollar and the euro meaning anything less than the wholesale collapse of the currency regime. After all who are the pretenders to the currency throne? Certainly not the yen. The Japanese are too insular to host the coin of the realm. The Swiss franc must contend with a banking system whose short-term bank debt equals 1,273% of the Swiss government's national debt. Clearly the gnomes of Zurich have been busy. By contrast, the U.S. looks positively chaste at 43%. (Source: New York Times; "The World's Banks Could Prove Too Big to Fail — or to Rescue'; 10/10/08; Floyd Norris.)

Best not to push too hard on that 43% figure though; according to Mr. Mortgage's recent calculations, American banks' so-called Level 2 'mark-to-market' balance sheet value approaches $7.3 trillion. As this number is a creature of Excel spreadsheets, the market-derived value could be anything, more likely significantly less. Mr. Mortgage's doom-laden prognostications have been pretty accurate since at least 2006.

In short, there are no bright beacons in the world. Fiats of all stripes have been done in by hubris. The loss of goodwill and trust in the power of paper --too hard to calibrate in the midst of the crisis-- will no doubt be staggering.

As for the Paulson Plan, it's an insult to band-aids everywhere. Apparently, the master plan is that all scorched parties must show up for future treasury auctions and pretend that their bandaged third-degree burns are mere flesh wounds. Isn't that the unspoken quid pro quo of the bail-out bill, uninterrupted Ponzi participation by foreign central banks? What dupe continues to show up for a Ponzi scheme after the pyramid's been revealed? The Plan reeks of global central bank fear. They will pretend on one another's behalf to avoid the eradication of their species. Our currencies are their hapless pawns.

Up until very recently, gradualists had held out hope for a long-term dollar-to-euro migration. However, this trail has become washed-out in recent days as the euro proves itself more committee than currency. This is extremely bad news for a world desperately in need of economic bipolarity. One implication of a dollar-saturated world is that safe havens get repealed. Every kitchen sink becomes one-step removed from a dollar. Getting from point A to B requires a dollar. Of course it's easy to parochialize the debate around those damnable dollars. The larger point is that the world is drunk on fiats: currencies, derivatives, stocks, bonds.

The currency will first be debauched until only a wheelbarrow full of it buys a cup of coffee. For one thing, influence purchased with sacks of gold is too susceptible to detection. Paper is the currency of epic-scale usury and malfeasance. Structured finance always had a Faustian ring. Seeking to defy God's laws of gravity and commensurateness it is, as Ezra Pound warned in 'With Usura', contra natura. We've been misstating our income and levitating our wealth. The world's elite are loath to face just how poor we – and they – are. For the populist, there may be a silver lining as the rich --by practical necessity financial-asset-bound-- have much further to fall than does the little guy. Thus the collapse of paper could have a laudatory distributive effect. No wonder Paulson sped through a $700 billion vacuum hose, affixing it to the coffers of Main Street. In order for the powers-that-be to avoid becoming the powers-that-were, they need us to re-capitalize them.

Moreover he $700 billion figure is hugely misleading. As the erudite blogger London Banker points out in his October 2 entry, $700 million is only the diameter of the spigot – like an income statement, a mere snapshot at any given time: "Whether the final value of the legislation this week is $700 billion or $150 billion is irrelevant as long as the laundering operation can accommodate the throughput, as that number is only a cap on total extensions at any one time."

Meanwhile the Great American Unipole is sick and getting sicker by the day. Absolute power has indeed corrupted absolutely. Iraq is the military facet of the same hubris. America succeeded beyond its wildest dreams, stuffing all gills with crappy Ponzi paper. The only solution available to the purveyors of paper is of course more paper; in short, a recipe for more disaster. Suddenly that industrial base looks like something more than a grimy anachronism. We make nothing, and the world is beginning to take notice.

Even a well-anticipated freight train is unavoidable when you're lashed to the track. The long-term answer must lie outside the fiat currency complex. But this is the Mount Everest of official denial. We will hyper-inflate back to a gold standard. No one in a position of power and authority will take us there. The currency will first be debauched until only a wheelbarrow full of it buys a cup of coffee. For one thing, influence purchased with sacks of gold is too susceptible to detection. Paper is the currency of epic-scale usury and malfeasance.

As it is, the world finds itself (much to its chagrin) divided into two sprawling camps: Americans and Americans-by-proxy (or if you prefer 'foreign bag-holders'). In short, both camps only pretend at being two camps. Together, they will slide, daisy-chained, into the abyss.

Europe's present turmoil marches the world one step closer to this abyss. Brazil and Argentina, God bless them, have announced bilateral trade will be conducted in their home currencies, no longer dollars. Of course they are less dollar-pregnant than Europe or China, economies who are frankly too big to bail --on the dollar. The euro was to be the world's second lifeboat. Hang on to your ciggies folks.

The Bid is the Father of the Ask

When risk conforms by profile or by sleights
of counter-party hand to prop a shoe
that cannot fall, or engineers a flight
to weaker hands --sound bid 's been bid adieu.

When ask splits distance that value can't divine
from hubris, moral compassing won't span
the gulf. Thus marked to market, we resign
to Fate which underwrites the boldest plan,

meting out peril rough to right reward,
and we meet our Maker on a cropless field
bankrupted by the grains we sought to hoard
and harvest. Then yield our epic greed

to untransacted glare undone by Him,
black swans and laissez-faire.

The poem 'Jaw-Boning' previously appeared at <u>The Wall Street Poet</u>.

Norman Ball

Metropolis, Ezra Pound, Mammon: And the Law of Too-Large Numbers

"The old world is dying away, and the new world struggles to come forth: now is the time of monsters."—Antonio Gramsci

(originally appeared in <u>Bright Lights Film Journal</u>, October 31, 2008)

[Author's Note: Though my thinking has changed somewhat, for the most part this essay could just as easily have been written today.]

Money Doctor Mario Draghi: "Europe is dying. The debt load proved too much."

The nation's leaders are struggling to address an insolvent investment banking system with prescriptive measures that sidestep Main Street's credit needs entirely. Gramsci's monsters have arrived, it appears, to ransack America through a series of bail-out monstrosities. But look at me, Ma, I'm quoting a venerable Marxist in this season of strange bedfellows. George Bush, cowboy capitalist-turned-Christian Socialist, is taking cues from *Un Hombre de Gentes*

Hugo Chavez. Intellectual consistency is dead. Long live chaos.

There's little risk of hyperbole when we concede the conceptual carnage wrought by the current avalanche of events is momentous and revolutionary. Few cherished concepts have weathered the onslaught. Alas, globalization was a euphemism for stuffing every corner of the global mattress with Ponzi paper. Financial intermediation, far from propagating efficient capital flows to Main Street, crowded out legitimate credit needs, bringing the commercial paper market to a grinding halt. Risk diversified itself alright — right into the shakiest hands — adding yet more stress to a precariously leveraged system. Economic interdependency extinguished safe havens. Greenspan's vaunted wealth creation was little more than asset inflation backfilled with debt. The platitudinous business cycle was usurped by a succession of bubble booms and busts, spurred on by what economist Eric Janszen has called the FIRE or finance, insurance and real estate economy. As asset values recede, the debt remains. The Party of Mao is the de facto lender of last resort to the U.S. Government, just as the latter is embarked on an aggressive nationalization campaign of its nation's banks and mortgage lending institutions. Confused yet?

If you want more evidence of tectonic form-shifting, listen to formally staid bodies such as the Bank for International Settlements (BIS) and the International Monetary Fund (IMF) expound upon looming abysses and financial Armageddons. Bankers are not prone to histrionics unless, of course, their world has tipped upside-down. Instructing on bank capitalizations and the delicate nature of the fractional reserve system, at least two recent CNBC commentators have made reference to the famous bank run in Capra's It's a Wonderful Life. George Bailey's heroic efforts presaged the Great Depression. Exactly how far are we to take this analogy?

As Hunter S. Thompson once remarked, "When the going gets weird, the weird turn pro." Tin-foil hats are suddenly haute couture. How delightful, though, that, for once, the elite's terror exceeds our own. This is because they have far more to lose from (gulp) equitable distribution due to financial collapse. Even during the fat times vast numbers of Americans were one paycheck away from destitution. Quiet desperation has always been built into the project. For now, poverty is loving the company as it stalks some unfamiliar and perfumed quarters while deep shit threatens to engulf us all in a stultifying classless society. Might both Marxes — Karl and Groucho — find room for satisfaction, scratching their beards in bemusement at the long strange tragicomic trip it all turned out to be?

Ronald Reagan's morning in America lasted right on through to dinner time. But the darkness is reassembling over the klieg lights. Fortunately, when the real gets surreal, the movies get mojo. Fritz Lang's *Metropolis* can best be described as a myopic dystopia. Richard Gilzean is right to say, "We do not look at Fritz Lang's silent films for any profound social meaning." Besides, wife and screenwriter Thea von Harbou was the programmatic Marxist of the pair.

Among many things, *Metropolis* misses the productivity gains of the computer age by a mile. Today's overclass no longer requires thousands of toiling laborers. However, the Illuminati wish to pass along a big thanks for the plebeian offer of continued toil on their behalf, cinematically at least. So Lang's futurism hasn't rendezvoused seamlessly with the future. We are becoming slaves to Gordon Gekko's Wall Street, not industrialism. Nonetheless, Lang's austere German Expressionist vision continues to evoke an angsty and unfocused dread that dovetails nicely with recent macroeconomic events.

To the unalloyed capitalist, when money ceases to exist, his world has, for all intents and purposes, ceased to exist along with it. What the plutocracy means, of course, is that their beloved fiat-stacked-atop-fiat complex is sliding into a financial asset abyss. Let's be clear. The world of real things is not in danger of being consumed by fire unless the resultant social unrest from financial asset meltdown creates real asset destruction (e.g. SUVs burnt in effigy), a plausible though collateral possibility.

Try imagining an I Am Legend corollary where the world is denuded, not of real people, but of investments bankers — Lehman Brothers' Dick Fuld and his ilk; a neutron-bombed landscape that leaves real assets standing while vaporizing all paper, computer hard drives, and electronic handshakes (credit derivative swaps (CDS) et al.). David Lynch would relish the narrative discontinuities of a moneyless world — Mulholland Drive without the wad of dough. Baudrillard might call it a hyper-reality bomb. Suffice to say a world without financial markets exceeds the grasp of most present-day minds.

Thus when you awake the morning after, your car is still in the driveway, the office buildings behind your house still stand, the power and water lines are all intact. Inquiring financial minds want to know, yes, but what are they worth? George Orwell said "to see what's in front of one's nose needs a constant struggle." Here's a reality that shouldn't require glasses, but often does: Economic value is inherently utilitarian. That is, when the received wisdom on value wanders from utilitarian metrics, markets have strayed into the realm of speculation, i.e., tulip country. Ever try eating a put option? Not in the abstract — say as a capital loss — but with ketchup. There are times when every good portfolio should have an ample stock of tuna fish — and an underweighting of collateralized mortgage obligations.

Are the meek on the verge of re-inheriting the earth? Those who kept faith with real things may be onto a windfall. America has an enviable supply of housing stock, real bricks and mortar stuff. One in ten homes built since 2000 is vacant. A financial holocaust? You bet. Shelter for the homeless? Of course, why not — if we can only shutter Countrywide's byzantine loss mitigation department and get to the real business of filling those houses. Given this surfeit of above-ground dwelling space, there's little need for Lang's subterranean sweatshop, unless, of course, we destroy the atmosphere, in which case it'll be the well-heeled who repair underground while the plebes toil away beneath a pitiless sun.

So don't let Ben Bernanke's existential fear infect you. A few field mice notwithstanding, the housing stock is not under siege. It's the financial superstructure (which, in fairness, allowed brick to be stacked upon superfluous brick in the first place) that's in peril of imminent demise. Soon it will be great to be real again. Soon real will be all we have left.

In an egalitarian world, Warren Buffet, that quirky billionaire who retained his modest suburban home — becomes even less distinguishable from everyone else. This is a populist's — if not a neo-Marxist's — wet dream. The radical curtailment or outright extinction of financial assets would be a tsunamic redistributive event; Rumplestiltskin's gold "de-alchemizing" back into straw. The bean counters have a name for it: financial de-leveraging. Last year, Satyajit Das, former Wall Street derivatives guru and author of Traders, Guns and Money, estimated each dollar of real capital supports $20 to $30 of loans. That's a lot of unwinding, not to mention a helluva lot of rich people.

Then there's the not-so-small matter of sheer scale. Ever try stuffing $1 billion under your mattress? Yes, the uber-rich have problems we can only dream of! Financial assets are both their lifeblood and their primary means of differentiation. Score one for an emboldened simple life as our class system looks increasingly to be constructed on the thinnest of airs and graces. Lang was right not to clutter the *Metropolis* landscape with an overly complex social structure. There have always been two essential camps: those who leverage the sweat of others and the sweaty others themselves.

As for the teeming underclass, does anyone really believe the whole world will accept 100 years of debt peonage to service what was essentially a financial phantom — ephemeral, "structured finance" instruments heaped beyond any sense of proportion to the world's intrinsic wealth? Try explaining to a French kid in 2100 that he can't have shoes because the decades-old hubris of some erstwhile Masters of the Universe on an entire other continent must be assuaged. Che Guevara could ride this sort of epic inequity with his eyes wide shut. Half the world would have to become enforcers because the rest will surely not submit to decades of servitude to pay off the greed of a tiny few.

When Europe's banking families facilitated the bankrupt royals of Europe, they were wise enough not to make the debt burdens existentially unattainable. Kings, no less than serfs, need to see some light at the end of the loan. A collapsing derivatives market — estimated in an October 12 Independent article at a staggering $516 trillion is analogous to the burst reservoir that engulfs *Metropolis'* subterranean city. Rising waters are impervious to class distinctions, drowning rich and poor alike. Indeed a number with nine (some say twelve) zeroes may lie beyond the reach even of the most rapacious hyper-inflation. It is a patently absurd figure in any context — ten times the annual GDP of the whole world. Even more absurd is to express this amorphous asset class in fiat currency form since, if it was ever to descend into the realm of transactional currency, it would submerge the most diligent printing press like a thousand-year flood. Scientific notation meets high finance — or high farce if you prefer.

Far better to repeal the financial order, re-calibrate the planes, trains, and automobiles in some as-yet unknown currency and START OVER. When greed broke bread with computer algorithms, it broke the bank. Now that same greed, leavened in no small measure by fear, bellows from some back room like Seymour in Little Shop of Horrors — feed me! Soon the storehouses will be empty like grain poured into an abyss.

The stage seems set for demagogues more than it does mediator figures in the vein of *Metropolis'* Feder. The young men of Wall Street, like the young men of *Metropolis*, have become effete and desperately out of touch. It's no small irony that Lang's initial inspiration for the *Metropolis* skyline was Manhattan. Grassroots global rage will coalesce as the initial panic subsides and people realize just how much they've been done unto. And they've been done unto a lot. During this Gramscian interregnum, various pretenders to the throne will emerge to galvanize billions of pissed-off humans; debt repudiation — or at least a disavowal of Main Street's peonage to credit derivative exposure — offers rich populist terrain. This much seems sure: Some violent re-assertion of the Real from beneath crushing numerical imaginariness will be attempted. Meanwhile, the poor old plutocracy, shrinking in numbers every day, will swear the anti-Christ is behind every bid to disavow derived wealth. Were Lang's Mediator to arrive at this particular inflection point, he would find the Brain lost in a maze of hubristic computer programs to which neither Brain nor Hands hold the upper hand. The world is buried beneath a Frankensteinian superstructure of electronic handshakes from which there is no certainty modern society will emerge intact. The better film analogy might be Kubrick's HAL 9000 — the computer as functional sociopath.

"The crisis," Gramsci wrote, "consists precisely in the fact that the old is dying and the new cannot be born: in this interregnum, morbid phenomena of the most varied kind come to pass." The original Paulson bail-out was a morbid symptom. Master of a Prior Universe, Hank Paulson (Frank Capra's Mr. Potter writ large) is striving mightily to breathe life into a corpse. Denial is the prevailing mindset of the elite. Without levered and derived wealth, their elite status is finished. They will enforce the bail-out with whatever means they have at their disposal.

Nelson Rockefeller would be heartsick at the New World Order's evolving socialist complexion. But this is not the heralded workers' revolt. As it turned out, a proletarian vanguard was hardly necessary. Good thing too, as they collect their soma every Friday night at Blockbuster Video and frankly couldn't seem to care less. Hurray for Hollywood! No, it was capitalism — biting off more of Ezra Pound's mammon than it could chew — that destroyed capitalism. The most sublime tragedy is tinged with irony. Wall Street, practicing a bastardized variant of capitalism, may destroy Main Street's more sociable capitalist model. To refute Wall Street's Gekko, greed is the sickness that swims through capitalism, not capitalism itself. The world may end not with a bang or a whimper, to paraphrase a famous Pound disciple, but rather in an orgy of Mammon.

In the aftermath of pathologic greed — prophesied by Ezra Pound — what third way looms on the horizon? It's possible we may muddle through a protracted Gramscian interregnum before a cohesive new system forms in the vacuum. As for *Metropolis*, it ends on a rather treacly note, everyone living blissfully mediated ever after. The same assurance hardly exists for a present-day world of biologic agents, suitcase nukes, and recalcitrant greed. Still, one can hope.

Far easier than speculating on what we will get is acknowledging what no longer exists. A traditionally stratified world will not accede peaceably to flatland status even if financial asset collapse all but assures a flatter landscape. So batten the hatches. Lang's atmospheric darkness, if not his journeyman Marxian storyline and climactic gush, fulfills its task well enough as cautionary tale.

The Invisible Hand's Invisible Hand Has a Thumb

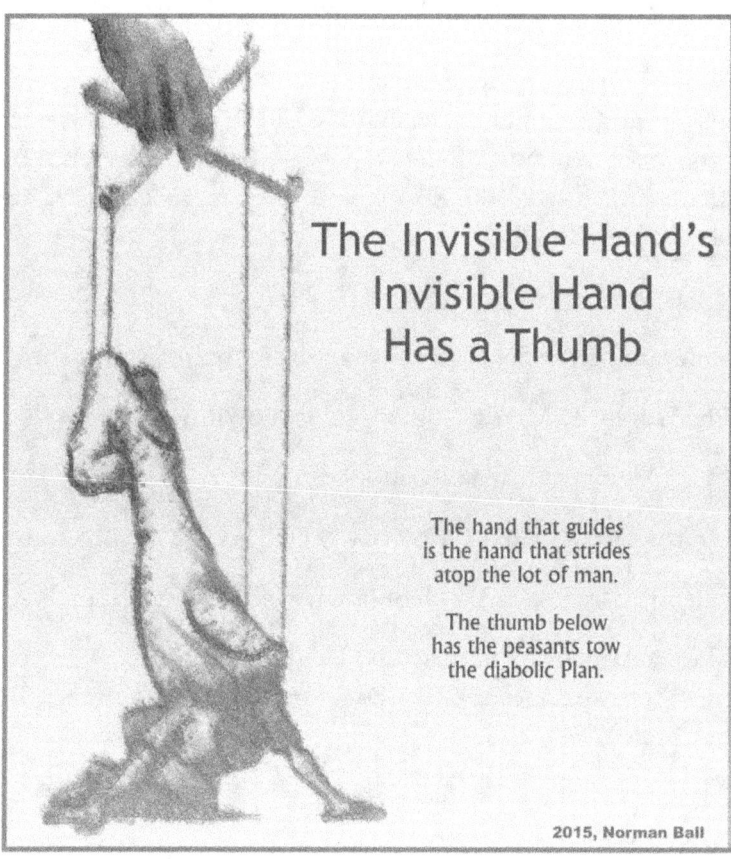

Bibliography

As should be obvious, this is not an academic work, but rather a collection of highly topical essays-of-the-moment collected into eBook form, only to 'get physical' as an afterthought. Much of what is cited here originates on a number of blogs by anonymous bloggers whose veracity, insight and thought leadership has either proven itself over time or is patently obvious. As this bibliography appears identically in both the eBook and the paperback, there are no URL's below.

Blogs (anonymous and not):

Vineyard of the Saker (www.vineyardsaker.blogspot.com)

Philosophy of Metrics (www.philosophyofmetrics.com)

FOFOA (www.fofoa.blogspot.com)

Dmitri Orlov's Club Orlov (www.cluborlov.blogspot.com)

Ellen Brown's Web of Debt (www.webofdebt.com)

Martin Armstrong' Armstrong Economics (www.armstrongeconomics.com/armstrong_economics_blog)

Alastair Crooke's Conflicts Forum (www.conflictsforum.org)

Henry C. K. Liu's collected essays and columns on Asia Times (www.atimes.com/atimes/Others/Henry.html)

Sheikh Imran Hosein on his personal website (www.imranhosein.org)

Henry Makow on his personal website

(www.henrymakow.com)

Redefining God (redefininggod.com)

Zero Hedge and its group of often-anonymous writers (www.zerohedge.com)

Damon Vrabel whose writings appeared at Financial Sense (www.financialsense.com)

Brandon Smith whose articles appear with regularity on Alt-Market (www.alt-market.com)

Bright Lights Film Journal (www.brightlightsfilm.com)

The Potomac: A Journal of Poetry and Politics (www. thepotomacjournal.com)

The Wall Street Poet (www.wallstreetpoet.wordpress.com)

Video Series:

Paul Grignon, Money as Debt, 2006

Damon Vrabel, Renaissance 2.0 – Financial Empire, 2010

Books:

Zbigniew Brzezinski, The Grand Chessboard: American Primacy And Its Geostrategic Imperatives, Basic Books; 1st edition (September 18, 1998)

Satyajit Das, Extreme Money: Masters of the Universe and the Cult of Risk, FT Press; 1 edition (August 17, 2011)

F. William Engdahl, <u>A Century of War: Anglo-American Oil Politics and the New World Order</u>, Progressive Press; New Rev Un edition (February 29, 2012)

Pepe Escobar, <u>Empire of Chaos: The Roving Eye Collection</u>, Nimble Books LLC (November 11, 2014)

Byung-Chul Han, <u>Transparency Society</u>, Herder (November 5, 2013)

Georg Wilhelm Friedrich Hegel, Werke. 2nd ed. Frankfurta. M.:Suhrkamp 1973, vols. 13– 15. (Theorie-Werkausgabe)

Ferdinand Lundberg, <u>The Rich and the Super-Rich: A Study in the Power of Money Today</u>, Lyle Stuart; 1st edition (June 1968)

George Orwell, <u>1984</u>, Signet Classic (July 1, 1950)

Karl Marx, <u>Das Kapital</u>, CreateSpace Independent Publishing Platform (March 2, 2011)

Warren Mosler, <u>The 7 Deadly Innocent Frauds of Economic Policy (MMT - Modern Monetary Theory Book 2)</u>, Amazon Digital Services, Inc., (February 16, 2015)

Jim Rickards, <u>The Death of Money: The Coming Collapse of the International Monetary System</u>, Portfolio; 1st edition (April 8, 2014)

Peter Dale Scott, <u>The American Deep State: Wall Street, Big Oil, and the Attack on U.S. Democracy (War and Peace Library)</u>, Rowman & Littlefield Publishers (October 30, 2014)

Orville Schell, <u>Wealth and Power: China's Long March to the Twenty-first Century</u>, Random House Trade Paperbacks (September 9, 2014)

Biography

NORMAN BALL (BA Political Science/Econ, Washington & Lee University; MBA, George Washington University) is a well-travelled Scots-American businessman, author and poet whose essays have appeared in Counterpunch, Asia Times, Foreign Policy Journal, The Western Muslim and elsewhere. His new book "Between River and Rock: How I Resolved Television in Six Easy Payments" is available here. Two essay collections, "How Can We Make Your Power More Comfortable?" and "The Frantic Force" are spoken of here and here, respectively. A collection of poetry "Serpentrope" is due out early 2014 from White Violet Press. He can be reached at returntoone@hotmail.com. Follow his Full-Spectrum Domino blog here.